# THE WOUND MAKES THE MEDICINE

## OTHER TITLES BY PIXIE LIGHTHORSE

# PIXIE LIGHTHORSE

# THE WOUND MAKES THE MEDICINE

REMEDIATIONS FOR
TRANSFORMING HEARTACHE

Cover illustration by Jillian Thalman

Library of Congress Cataloging-in-Publication Data Available Upon Request

ISBN 978-1-955905-43-5 (TP)

ISBN 978-1-9559-0544-2 (eBook)

Printed in the United States

Distributed by Simon & Schuster

First Edition

10 9 8 7 6 5 4 3 2

*This ceremony of life*
*in which we kill the little untruths over and over*
*to save the big truth of love that lives within us*
*Sit up for the ceremony!*
*Love cannot exist without the justice of healing*

# CONTENTS

# DEAR READER

THESE WRITINGS ARE THE PIECES OF ME THAT ROSE UP during deep healing after a shattering heartbreak touched off many older, yet-unhealed heartbreaks. It would not be fair to speak in detail about the catalyst, for straws that break camels' backs are merely tipping points that reveal where too many assumptions have been allowed to shape a life. I am guessing that you know what I'm talking about: It begins with feeling like something is a little off, and realizing that "off" feeling is connected in a weblike way to many other little incongruencies and concessions—tiny self-betrayals that amass in a mob to rip out whatever version of the picket fence we've constructed.

New grief has a way of stirring up ancient grief. In the process of refusing to go cold in my heart, deciding to stay with myself through the pain and the reality, and titrating the flow of intense emotions, I found strange medicine being made right in my mind and body, by my pain. I made countless voice memos to remind myself of what was happening to me—desperate love letters from the future I could not yet sense that would make their way into the writing that appears here. I could not do anything with them at the time, but they were waiting for me when I made it back to the shore.

When my marriage ended, my heart was perched upon the familiar ledge so many of us face when we lose those tenderest elements we believed belonged to us, the daily nutrients that were taken for granted when we were partially living in a fantasy—ingredients like love, intimacy, connection, vulnerability, security, safety, predictability, trust, hope, and desired outcomes we so hoped for based on positive projections and potential. Good and spirited love built with grand expectations cannot withstand storms when built on quaking foundations of unhealed, unacknowledged trauma.

I live and work on a ranch in the high desert of the Pacific Northwest, where the workdays are long and each adult carries a double load. It was a mild winter that year, thankfully, yet I cannot remember taking my coat off. My throat stayed wrapped in a moth-eaten scarf as I jaggedly walked from chore to chore, not quite numb and often crying. Tears cleanse us—not of uncleanliness, but by offering a sterile flush for open wounds. That's because they contain the perfect ratio of salt for battered emotions. Weeping was infection prevention for me, and in that time, I became acutely aware of how little weeping I had done in my life. It was debilitating and disabling, and it dawned on me that we have developed a lexicon for mental-health issues in this so-called culture, yet we do not have sufficient language (at least not in English) for emotional disabilities, just as we do not have much space at all for grief. The overculture (dominant culture that creates social norms—and punishes those who do not live by them) does not offer rituals and resources for the brokenhearted. Only distractions and numbing agents, affirmational Post-it Notes that do not stick long to dusty mirrors.

I was torn between the chores of parenting, preparing meals, and tending the land's never-ending needs. As I felt along my ripped edges, I sensed my untimely rage and my desire for control over the way this relationship was ending that was tearing me apart, even as it challenged me to stay open and remain with myself. I had to surrender the control that had helped me create such intricate armor around me.

It was a sacred privilege to be with my grief—and it was a choice. It was not indulgent. It was a long ceremony filled with visions, nightmares, ancestral horrors, and shit-fit wars with my ego. I battled with fixation on external factors, seeking outlets for my disappointment, frustration, disgust, and annihilation. I walked aboveground by day, as necessary, and I swam in my darkness for eleven months. I struggle for language to describe being in two worlds devoid of identity, floating between the mundane and the existential. Words would not come for weeks, until I managed to stitch myself up; and for several-day periods, there would be what my comrade called "fire in my face"—and then I would go gray again. I could not predict how big the waves would be or when they would overtake me. Old shadows and family legacy burdens haunted my sleep, and I could not remember, nor conjure the hunger, to eat.

Harrowing experiences of emotional rupture impact many of us, especially in these times of collapse we're collectively in. During my medicine-making period, I began to see how I felt, according to the language with which most of us are familiar. The overculture calls it depression or dissociation, but it also goes by many other names, some of which you've probably already heard. Some are helpful for a time—others, not so much. At their worst, our labels and names for things create limits. We're learning that we are infinite—that our range is beyond naming, that our fixity is not real, that language is designed to help us share our experience as best we can.

I felt my body changing as I moved with disabling heartbreak. My being, as I had come to know it, transformed, recovered, and healed, as my ancient wounds decided they could trust me to see them as they truly were. I assembled the fragments of myself that were coming back together in my awareness in accordance with the elements—fire, water, earth, and air. Each had their way with me as I walked another splintered suspension bridge of internal emotional instability. Fire warmed me and burned my house down. Water quenched and held me under until I drowned. Earth gave me her plants to heal, and her vines strangled my old way of being. Air breathed me whole by day and held a pillow over my face at night. All were teachers with shadow sides that mirrored the option to self-sabotage, to stay encased in the unhealed parts of my proud flesh.

This book uses the elements to demonstrate how, when we are in grief and pain, we tend to live inside the properties of the elements themselves. Sometimes it feels like we're burning, or drowning, or buried alive, or getting the wind sucked out of us. There are contrary medicines for each of these elemental influences: releasing and transforming, surrendering and floating, grounding and connecting with nature, breathing full deep breaths and reconnecting to the oxygen of life. For me, the processes are not linear, even though they are arranged in order of each of the elements (and preceded by "proud flesh," which describes the context of the body-in-healing that contains all the elements, too).

I scrawled through the pages of my journal when I felt I was drowning in complex emotions, and I found ways to surrender to the waves and become a proficient surfer. Inflamed with anger about what I couldn't control when my relationship house was burning down, I carried the pointed sticks close to my chest and hugged them tightly with love for the lessons I was determined to learn. I placed them in the fire as an offering, with prayers to release. When I felt the air punched out of me by betrayal, I challenged the places where my windpipes felt choked and caught, and focused on my whole breaths for days at a time while I literally chopped firewood and did the chores of three people. When I felt buried alive, trapped underground by my grief, I let the earth compost me and envisioned medicinal plants sprouting from my skeletal remains.

Each element has the power to give life or take it away. In my most painful periods, I die. In my most uplifted, I am slowly reborn. Another spiritual awakening has thus far delivered resuscitation, leaving it up to me to mind what has more power than me, to respect the forces of nature long before I entertain decision-making on the bases of fears, ideals, and dreams alone. Failure does not come from making mistakes, but from not learning their lessons.

This is not a book about a marriage ending or the loss of a grandiose dream, but of everything loss sets off inside us and time calls us to finally tend to. The essays within are to be read at your leisure, in whatever order you wish; you might even open the book at random and find the medicine that has synchronously summoned you. The affirmation at the end of each piece is the medicine for breathing in and meditating with as you tend your own wounds that time is calling you to heal. Journal with them if you feel called to create descriptions around the sensations and releases that arise. It can be healing to describe the experience, and then come back to your writing later to see if the description still fits. It is also okay to recognize that words are inherently limiting, and not all processes need documentation in order to impact you.

I want to share in the language I have at my disposal to conjure what a body and heart can do when they release the mind's desire to control that which it cannot. I have unscrewed the lid to show you the rich, viscous, oily, life-affirming salve that heartache can make of our real-time and ancestral pain. Mine is rustic and roughly scented, like bear tallow whipped smooth, with bits of root, blood, and eviscerated bone, softened in the mortar and pestle of surrender. It will cure over time, and I will continue to add to it. Yours will be different, with sensuous and ambrosial qualities made for you, by you.

Please note that the lyrics in this songbook are not a "how to" as much as a "walks with." If I had written this book as poetry, as I originally wanted to, I would have tucked my feelings and experiences into noxious yet floral verses containing cryptic instructions for how to avoid feeling profoundly foolish and alone! Another time, maybe. At any rate, my desire was to tenderly touch our scars and find ways to speak to them without objectifying, exploiting, or dominating the pain we all feel.

Loss is death, and losing something or someone of great importance challenges us to get very close with nature, as well as our innate nature, to heal. This book begins with a section titled "Tending Scar Tissue" to remind you of the results of our tender, formative years becoming slowly armored with layer upon layer of scar tissue over hurt, and to where we return when we are confronted with potential or further heartbreak. Fortunately, we need not end in more armor. That's no way to live, and we cannot take it with us when we die. Becoming discerning, self-trusting, self-loving, self-wanting, and disarmed is a journey through the many elements and epiphanies that loss introduces us to. With practice, even our fixation with "self" begins to fall away. In the midst of our aching and yearning, we carry the brush fires, tidal waves, earthquakes, and gale-force winds of nature within our personal ecosystems. There is pain, chaos, and destruction here—but also the ingredients for healing, renewal, and new possibilities for beauty and hope.

My aspiration is that your own walk through the creative, destructive, renewing journey with heartache makes the medicine you need most. May you travel around the wheel of elements in a circular manner—through a labyrinth of tenderness, rage, passion, waves, salt, humus, and breath—to be a fool for love in all forms and wise enough to stay connected to your heart at all costs.

*Love,*
Pixie

# PROUD FLESH

*Scars form*

*sinuous and silky*

*tenacious tissue*

*to cover and protect*

*the torn*

# TENDING SCAR TISSUE

DEAR HEART, YOUR PROUD FLESH IS SCAR TISSUE THAT grew over your wounds—more than what was needed to heal properly. It formed thick and substantial on the surface over the energy of your capacity to love and be loved, an overprotective armor that cannot yet trust the air to heal it. It protrudes—raised, uneven, and excessive.

It is understandable that defensive armor results from trust and love disappearing without your consent, taken from you without your control or desire to release it—and yet, exposure to your awareness is what it needs to reawaken to the flow of your blood. Proud flesh doesn't want to have needs. It is a trauma response that choked out the possibility for you to be loved the way you yearned to be loved.

Heartache is the midwife that can birth you into new levels of healing . . . with your permission. The cost of staying hidden beneath thick scars impacts all of your relationships, the work you choose to do in the world, how roughly or gently you nurture children, the voice you use to "discipline" yourself to keep on living.

The proliferation of tissue that overgrows your wounds is tough by design, and it must be broken down with care, exposed to sunlight and warmth, tenderized gently but consistently to be integrated back into the body. In your armored state, you must find all the ways to consent to be vulnerable to light and air. Being outside where the sun can fall on your face and warm your bones—while you acknowledge where in your body the hurt is crying silently—is a simple act of dissolution that nature provides. Speaking to a trusted friend, drawing your loved ones close, and learning who can witness you in your fluid and ever-changing moods without judgment can prepare your system for transformation.

Healing your deepest cuts requires your determination to permit the healing to take place within you; to replace your fear with a stronger desire to risk loving and being loved, which includes being injured by love again and again; to be intimate with your body and your life as they are right now, which requires giving up the ghosts that have taken up residence here.

Energetically, proud flesh holds fast, stopping your breath before it can reach all areas of your body. It is my consistent experience that my breath will come up from my diaphragm and catch right where I hold my fear—just at my sternum, midway between my navel and my heart. During my periods of freezing up and fighting my cycle of inner healing, I needed to challenge that catch. I envisioned it as a small pair of jaws that clamped my windpipe each time my body sought breath.

I want all of my breath, in all the places my body needs it. I want you to want yours, too. It is our birthright to breathe completely. Part of the sacred task of transformation is challenging ourselves to return to profound love, which will gradually soften the scar tissue that armors us.

*I am called to expose the battered fragments of my heart to light and air, trusting that nature knows best how to move me forward.*

# STAYING WITH THE ACHE

It is possible to release control, surrender, and be open to an outcome different from the one you had hoped for. Don't try to go at a pace faster than what you can handle. Simplify. Put your "big plans" on hold.

You cannot make many plans apart from simply being with the ache. The ache will tell you everything you need to know, while fear will try to talk loudly over it. Fear often says that if you stay present with your pain, you will get stuck in it. Fear says that once you open the floodgates, you may not be able to stop the pain from surging through.

Why are we afraid that if we allow ourselves to feel the depth of our pain, we will get sucked into a lifelong depression? I believe that some states deemed by the overculture to be negative and unwanted come from a denial of what hurts. How will denying our hurt move the needle forward?

You must allow yourself to feel your heartache, so that you can be reclaimed by the healing that comes after the worst has been fully felt. Underneath the pain of today's loss is yesterday's untended hurt, hopelessness, and disappointment . . . asking to be acknowledged, to be fully felt.

If emotional pain were a soft-tissue injury, the ligaments around the injury site would need gentle lengthening, so the tissue could breathe and become fluffy and pink again. Toughened scar tissue was not given a chance to be rehabilitated at the time of injury. It now requires extra care, patience, and slow movement so circulation can flow again.

*I will work gently and slowly with the old pain awakened by today's pain, to soothe the original injuries that caused me to hurt so much.*

# BEING PRESENT
# AND SETTING BOUNDARIES

Your healing process will not stand for controlling or rigid agendas. It does not call for bullying from the parts of the self that want to hurry the process along, or anxious attempts to accept the hurt and be done already. It will not stand for being filed away, but rather will petition patiently through inconsistent sensations and ever-changing emotions, and the natural ebb and flow of noticing, which will sometimes entail confusion or agony. It needs your devoted attention.

These moments of confusion and agony may feel never-ending, but they will wane with love and proper care. You might unconsciously suspend loving yourself if it seems too hard under the circumstances. Perhaps you're working through guilt or old shame . . . but it's still possible to love and honor yourself, as well as the slow process of healing.

I encourage you to set boundaries for what you do and do not have energy for. I find that interacting with people when I am really hurting is challenging, so I set limits on my interactions, as well as what I bring to and seek from them. It is important to maintain an inward focus in times of pain. We do not think of heartbreak as a listening time, as a prompt to surrender deeply to what is flowing through us. We are accustomed to collapsing, or tucking things away to deal with later, or giving all our time to people and situations outside ourselves.

In this medicine-making stage, we must look into our hurts and be present to them. There is a desperation that comes with unjust loss and a very physical sensation that can feel overwhelming at times. Your body and soul have had to withstand a lot to get to this place of tending torn heartspace. May your wholeness be fed with consistency of care, and cradled by the process itself, as well as by your willingness to be deeply present with it.

*I will allow myself to surrender to the hurt and set limits and boundaries around my resources so that I can stay with the process.*

# TAKING BACK OUR PROJECTIONS

YOUR PROUD FLESH WILL INEVITABLY BUMP UP AGAINST the proud flesh of others. What I mean by this is that the feelings you cannot tolerate will show up as projections you wish others to hold for you. A projection is nothing more than a defense mechanism that you subconsciously use to cope with painful feelings. We seek to target others to get out of working with the pain they triggered. For example, perhaps you are experiencing rage that doesn't seem safe to feel—maybe you end up perceiving your partner or another loved one as being wrathful and angry all the time, and you accuse this person of torpedoing your life with hot temper. There may be a grain of truth to your perception . . . but there may also be an aspect of you that doesn't want to claim its own part in the dynamic. Likewise, as you go through your own process of healing, you might face other people's projections; they might tell you to "get over it" or suggest that you're too intense, because some unhealed part of them is "too intense," hasn't moved through their pain, and requires their attention, care, and love.

We often do this with one another: dance with versions of hurtful truths placed on one another's altars in the hopes that the other will take them on. This is a misguided form of "care." When others take our projections on, our interactions become more complex and more painful.

In the dance of projections, we go round and round until we hit something that threatens our relational container. We become stuck in a feedback loop of undisrupted patterns that create constant tension and drain us of our vitality. Fights with partners, children, friends, and between different parts of ourselves are exhausting, and often drag us into a desperate desire for dramatic action.

When we are dealing with projections—the ones we fling onto others or the ones they fling onto us—it becomes hard to keep our ears and hearts open. Often, we do not possess the language, the calmness, or the skills to navigate the war of my experience over yours. We wear out and want to throw in the towel.

Most of us, even those of us navigating the realm of healing, have been taught that surviving means fighting. But the battle we are waging is for the purpose of taking back our power, our agency, our clarity—and with that, we must include our projections. Circling back into unhelpful patterns that cause us to be hypervigilant and hyper-individualistic is not gentle, forward-motion progress toward healing. Staying locked in emotional and behavioral patterns that keep us engaged in fight mode eventually strangles relationships. Putting our unhealed, untreated, unexamined "stuff" on someone else harms everyone involved.

You can learn how to track and disrupt your patterns of projection by looking back at your internal relationship with yourself and your relational history with others—and call yourself and others to the table in a caring way that will help you grow, not send you spiraling through shame and blame.

Mingled with the pain you are suffering today, there are projections you've internalized and taken into yourself . . . and that you've put on others to avoid your own pain. Let your current pains be an invitation—a clarion call that is alerting you, so that you can give your care and attention to something deeper within you that longs for lasting healing.

*I reclaim the projections I've placed on others and allow the parts of me that are in pain to be acknowledged and healed.*

# WELCOMING THE DARKNESS

HEARTACHE BIRTHS HEALERS. HEALERS STUDY SHADOWS and desolate places within themselves. Healers worth their salt study their inner darkness at great length. This process must not be hurried. The arc of time enables you to become humble enough to share your experiences with others.

Humility claims us and is demonstrated through our behavior. We do not wave it like a flag. False humility is common among those of us who are still moving from insecurity. Humility is not a permanent state; it is always being challenged. When my defenses arise, I am in a battle with fragile parts of my ego. Because trauma results in anxiety and insecurity, humility is not a goal as much as the natural outgrowth of challenging our defenses and making choices from vulnerability rather than hurt.

Do not confuse darkness with badness, or evil. Darkness is the residence of all liminal spaces: the womb, the cave, the unacknowledged wisdom that is your task to unearth. Your ancestors have provided you with the tenacity to be here today, to tend your own heart—and you also cultivate fortitude of heart by living the life you have right now. Your heart is a hearth in which you bring the kindling of your sufferings close to your chest. Your sufferings are fuel for the fire—and bringing them to your heart, the center of you, prepares your body for release.

Your wounds are hard at work making their sacred medicine in the hidden spaces below the scars. With loss, there may be nothing satisfying for you to reclaim. If a special person has died, or love went away, what we yearn for most is an impossible return. The sacred task at hand is to let yourself be reclaimed by something deeper than the immediacy of struggle and pain. This something need not be identified or fixated upon, but surrendered to.

What does investing in your partnership with healing look like to you? Being birthed into new ways is painful, but it is a blessing to be transformed—to be rebirthed after an ordeal wherein a ravenous beast has digested your pain in one of its thousand cosmic stomachs. The beast's roots crawl for your feet while the sky blows windstorms against your meat and up your bony spine, sucking poison like a hurricane sucks up palm trees. It sounds dramatic, and allowing ourselves to change deeply ingrained patterns can be dramatic. This is why our body will do whatever it can to get our attention.

Change starts right here, in the dark, sacred, unseen processes of our bodies—where we feel, sense, trust, and know; and where we can create conditions for improved states of being without force by accustoming ourselves to the contours of the depths that we hold, and that hold us in turn.

*I trust the darkness and its specific luminosity, which helps me see and recognize my familiar patterns—and to heal them without intellectualizing, defining, categorizing, or overanalyzing them.*

# WALKING IN THE LIMINAL

LIMINAL SPACE IS USED TO DESCRIBE THE AREA BETWEEN two defined territories: the in-betweenness just before dawn when the day hasn't yet come alive, and just after dusk when we do not yet consider it nightfall. Liminality is not limbo or nothingness; there are no decisions to be made here, simply the state of being in the unknown that we find in the midst of transition.

Liminality accompanies the struggle felt in uncertainty; before we make any decisions or commitments, we have the healing potential to be with the broken fragments of our heart with as much calm attention as possible. To attune to the heart is to sympathize with it.

I feel this state mostly just before waking, when my dreams are still fuzzy and I am closest to the forces of nature that hold me when I'm resting the deepest, yet possessing just a bit of lucidity and consciousness. Being in this space can feel frustrating, because we are oriented to always be doing something. In liminal space, there is nothing to be done, no pressure to "accomplish" anything. Still, when heartbreak and disappointment are upon you and it seems as though there is no end in sight, it can feel frustrating to be unable to shift your state. You may be wondering when there will be relief from all this suffering; or you may wish that you knew what action to take that would remove you from this purgatory.

It is not only time that heals wounds, but a complex and flavorful broth of love, reflection, a willingness to be with the truth of what caused the pain—and when the pain occurs, the ability to release it to healing. Your broken heart doesn't call for management. It is not a business. It does not need unending, silent suffering, masks, or pretending. It howls for gentle companionship with your consciousness, like a lonesome wolf in a graying, misty canyon. Simply letting yourself be in the tender fog of your becoming will eventually help you to step over the threshold and move into the next phase, when the moment is right.

*I give myself grace to stay in the uncomfortable in-between spaces, and to find beauty and peace in allowing myself to be.*

# HONORING GRIEF
# IN THE COMPANY OF OTHERS

IN HARDSHIP AND STRUGGLE, YOU STAGGER BROKEN and empty-handed in and out of the land of death and through disappointment, abuse, and fear, with a sense that the only way to remain standing is not to lie down. Loss and heartache feel as if something has died, and many times, something *has* died. In this state between resistance and acceptance, we masquerade as though everything is fine. It is too hard to explain what is happening inside of us.

I do not prefer to tell my agonies to everyone I meet, and so I, like you, have learned to smile through the pain so that others don't worry about me. Of course, some of this entails denying what's really happening and what I'm really feeling, as all of us are deeply conditioned to put on a happy face, pull up our bootstraps, keep a stiff upper lip, and temporarily dismiss or minimize how exhausted and shattered we are on the inside. The overculture does not allow us to openly show our grief.

In this year of transformation from agony to acceptance and release, my skin looked pasty and gray most days. I couldn't remember if I showered, and I didn't really care. From anxiety comes ambivalence; after all, the only way to pause the pain cycle is to stop caring. The contradiction is exhausting. I chopped wood and carried water, avoided people as much as possible, and tried not to visibly bring my burdens into shared space. When I couldn't hide it, I received more compassion than I expected, but I wondered if it was genuine. Was I creating compassion fatigue among my comrades by dragging this never-ending torment like a smelly bag of laundry into their personal space?

There is deep insecurity in us when it comes to burdening and bothering others with our troubles. Some aspects of isolation were healing for me, and others felt complicit with what we are conditioned to accept: that wearing our pain makes us miserable company.

Proud flesh is already complex without having to layer it with phony smiles and fear masquerading as self-sufficiency. How you act is up to you, and people who cannot tolerate the duration of your transforming pain may not be your people. It can be surprising to see who stays to witness grief, and who disappears. It is important to honor that not everyone has the capacity to see you through the dark nights, and to be grateful for those who do.

*I will participate in transforming myself and the overculture by honoring my grief in my community without shame.*

# LEANING INTO THE ANCESTORS

HEALING HEARTACHE CALLS FOR REINFORCEMENTS. IF you don't feel strong, you can invite perseverance from all available sources to disrupt legacy burdens (or ancestral struggles) of internal pain that get fired up by new pain. Often, our grief reminds us of what lies hidden in the body's archives, from not just this lifetime but the lifetimes of our ancestors. I borrow strength from my ancestors when I am weak with pain and heartache. They are a source of endurance—and I know this because I am here.

It is not necessarily a close affinity I have with them, as much as a remembrance that they made a space for me to be born that I can lean into. Leaning into the ancestors is challenging when all we recall of them is how hard their lives were. When I become fixated on legacy burdens, which I may be feeling as a result of how patterns pass down through genetics and conditioning, I deprive myself of their joy.

All of our ancestors had songs and music as part of their culture, just as we do. The spirituals, hymns, prayers, medicine songs, and energetic melodies that are held by the cultures of our families of origin help us to build stamina and to heal. Legends live inside them. Messages of survival and thriving are hidden in our ancestral songs. If you reach behind you for help and you do not find it, reach further back. There will be a time in your genetic history when the joy of your people is strong and their hearts can still be sensed. Let it guide you to your core.

It's been said that karma isn't a curse, but simply fear that repeats in your mind and goes unchallenged. It's time to face that fear, to challenge it with love, a courageous heart, and a loud, if shaky, voice. It's time to be the ancestor that future generations will call upon when they, too, are in need of a reminder of their own deep strength.

*I recognize that my ancestors are sources of wisdom—and they have lessons to share that transcend suffering and teach me the meaning of joy.*

## ACTING AS OUR OWN
## FIRST RESPONDER

WHEN YOU HONOR HURT AND CONFUSION, YOU OPEN
to the medicine that helps you heal. When I feel pain, even
if it's just from smashing my finger, my instinct is to recoil
and resist. Fear that I have done serious damage creates
constriction and sends my pain receptors into a tizzy. I ease
sudden physical pain with deep, calming breaths—closing
my eyes and allowing panic to slow so I can use my thinking brain to remember to get my first-aid kit.

Emotional pain often comes with confusion, and those
two together can create resistance. Just knowing they go
together and that our more deeply hurt parts throb with
resistance is sometimes enough to release the fear and tension for a moment of reprieve, so we can seek the kind of
first aid our heart needs.

If you have been lacerated by abuses of abandonment,
neglect, rejection, betrayal, infidelity, or anything else, listen for what your pain needs. Then, you can stand over the
warming brew of your transgressions, your unhealed hurts,

your parts that are still asking for forgiveness, and be a caring first responder.

If you feel tempted to abandon your own healing process when fear and resistance overtake you, try to envision the medicine that wants to come into form. Nature and imagination can remind you of what this medicine feels like. Can it be found in sensory experiences of sound, taste, scent? What self-healing ointment is made for you when you take yourself into nature?

I find parts of my remedies in the early-evening serenade of the sunset-shouldered, red-winged blackbird—that cosmic techno song speaks to my soul in ways for which I have no words! Can you hear the steady hush of the wind over the rooftops as you lie alone in your shadows—the same way you have heard it so many times before, the same way it will carry on for thousands of more years? With your senses, try to take in all nature's messages: where she glides, graceful and ethereal, and where she plummets, full of gravity and longing. Nature holds complexity in a way that can inspire us; she holds every permutation of sensation, emotion, and possibility, and she is also drenched with unmerciful suffering.

Your connection to nature promises new life—alongside and because of pain. Two or more seemingly opposing realities can exist at once. Nature's medicine plays a prominent role in our lives, demonstrating life and death, seasonal changes, predators and prey, sunrises and sunsets—cycling with what seems like ease, even in her dramatic displays. When you listen for what your pain needs, you see that your agony is innately tied to your peace and joy.

Your willingness to connect to yourself and the world around you sets you on a path of connection with all that is. Look in the mirror and at other beings with your spirit eyes—illuminated beams that have peered into the horrors of existence, as well as unfathomable beauty. May the parts that still ache trust-fall backward into the pits of despair, with the willingness to be purified in the furnace of your pain. Remember that your liberation begins inside, and can be supported by the cycles of nature moving in and around you.

*I act as my own first responder by listening for harmonies in the coexistence of profound beauty and immense pain.*

# LETTING FOOD
# BE OUR MEDICINE

WHEN YOU'RE IN THE THROES OF HEARTACHE, YOU MAY care less about nutrient-rich food than when you feel well. It can be a time of either shutting down your appetite or stress eating. Either way, your whole system is affected by heartbreak.

It's possible to shut off the signals from your brain telling you when it's time to eat. This can create a host of secondary issues that affect your health. Skipping meals or eating non-nutrient-dense food is common as you undergo pain and move through the slow healing process. It is most important to find the will to gain nourishment from food when you're in an acute state of mourning and loss, or under the consistent daily influence of anxiety and depression. Eating three times a day with healthy snacks between meals can keep your body in service to your heart as it mends.

It is holy medicine to seek the foods of your ancestors. For me, this looks like mushing and shaping the wetted, pale masa into rectangles that will hold the shredded venison; that will shelter the black-eyed peas and the road-side greens from the ditch that borders the old cemetery; that will humbly house the dent corn grown in this very ground in a soft pillow wrapped in husk, which will roll into something that often gets mistaken for a tamale, which will then gently turn my lips into an unforced smile, bringing an easeful joy even as I feel myself wilting in loneliness.

You know how this goes—this process of being with multiple truths at one time. Being with complexity is part of maturing and growing through difficulty. We can feel the pain that drains us of our will to go on, alongside the simple joy that comes from nourishing ourselves.

All your separated parts swell with life force when you honor the food of your people and your soul this way. It is possible to transform your way of being when you eat like your ancestors did. The nature of healing calls for cell food and soul food, and nature provided exactly what your ancestors needed to survive and thrive for thousands of years. I have found that eating from my ancestors' traditional plates is like taking in their spirits, which strengthens me as I learn to walk a path forward and away from pain.

For now, while you may not be able to have what you want, you can reclaim something you need.

*I nourish myself with the foods of my people to gain the strength to fully be with the challenges I am facing.*

# LISTENING TO
# THE BODY'S STORIES

YOUR BODY IS WISE BEYOND YOUR KNOWING. IT CONTAINS messages that become clearer and more resonant as you move deeper into healing. I've experienced these messages as complaints from the areas of my body that store trauma. From the jumpiness of my mercilessly over-tickled ribs to the buzzing ball of fear in my solar plexus to my chronically sore throat to my ankle that repeatedly pronates—these are memos that appear the more I seek healing.

It is sometimes hard to accept that my body has so many stories to tell about where I was hurt, couldn't stand on my own two feet, had my voice shut down, and became terrified of chaotic emotions that arose from too much happening too fast. Our miraculous systems learn early on how to adapt to stress in all its forms. It's as if we tuck parts of ourselves away that cannot bear more emotional stress and damage. We fracture into pieces and temporarily forget these parts in order to survive the moment.

This is a form of dissociation, a term used to describe how we cut ourselves off from emotions too powerful to fully experience at the time they occur. It is a coping mechanism that mitigates the pain we feel. It may seem like a good idea to tuck unwanted emotions down into the depths, but as we grow older, we need more of our emotions to be present so that we can function more highly in our relationships, our jobs, and our care of children and elders.

Listening to your body for patterns and requests can give you clues about where some of the fractured parts have hidden themselves to stay safe. I find that if I want to shut down a difficult conversation or try to speak the truth with vulnerability, I get a painful lump on the right side of my throat. When I fear betrayal, the bees start buzzing loudly in my solar plexus, ready to defend against an attack. These are trauma responses, and our bodies tend to store them in places that become more difficult to ignore as we mature. Removing the armor when I am in fear is becoming a higher priority as I grow older, as I long for healthier responses to turmoil, as well as transparency and continuity in my relationships.

Old pain that is activated by new pain (often signaled by scratched-upon memories) is a signal to dig deeper within myself, knowing that the current situation might be a catalyst but not necessarily the cause. I want to ask myself what the relationship is between these two hardships so that I may identify what is chronic for me and what I need to bring attention to.

Dissociating cuts you off from such gentle inquiries, as it causes you to armor your heart and reject the wisdom that you contain in your body to care for yourself. It is a reflexive response involving little care and consciousness for what your body actually needs. We can create more harm for ourselves and others in this state, causing our situation to become even more layered with complexity and the need for cleanup. We are always being asked by the systems we live under to sweep our needs under the rug and keep going. Accepting the body's wisdom to identify and bring coherence into the harmed and hurting places is a necessary investment in ourselves and our most important relationships.

*I notice when my body is giving me helpful information about what needs to heal.*

# ADDRESSING OUR DISCOMFORT

Our culture worships comfort and requires us to deny what is uncomfortable—to manipulate, medicate, and numb in order to avoid discomfort and keep moving. It is much easier to sell products to people who are willing to ease discomfort with pseudo comforts.

We pad our lives with fluffiness so the sharpness cannot be felt. That's why becoming intimate with our personal pain by allowing ourselves to feel it fully, to see how it has impacted us in an embodied way, is so important: It allows us to take responsibility rather than remain manipulated by forces outside ourselves that ultimately do not care about our well-being. Taking responsibility for our pain can mean being with the felt sensations, with how they show up in our psyche and body, before seeking solutions.

For many emotions and experiences, there are no sufficient words to describe them. We do the best we can to communicate to others what this heartache is like, but it is multidimensional and private, and sometimes defies language and the constructs of "healing" that are too often thrown at our pain as quick-fix solutions. To honor our scars, we have the opportunity to push back on the inherent limitations of the tools we have been given to create quick resolutions and move on. In this convenience-addicted society, where "easy" solutions to our problems are ubiquitous, I do not know of a single product that can transform heartbreak.

There is a particular kind of divine beauty in being dissolved, dismembered, and disarmed that is not exactly marketable. It is not touted as a solution because it cannot be packaged and sold. Healing is an art that defies categorization.

The process of sitting and massaging your scar tissue, releasing the metaphorical fascia that has become bound with hurtful experiences, tending them, writing about them, releasing them—all of this is cathartic and in direct opposition to how we are acculturated.

Staying with our heartache is an act of radical resistance. It causes us to dispense with the need for false comfort and pretend solutions. It means that we will not be working around the clock to distract ourselves and spend money on items that do not serve our deeper healing but instead leave us spinning in the hamster wheel of our trauma, perpetuating the suffering that is crying out for our personal attention and kind ministrations.

Choosing to be with yourself as you transform through heartache is an act of justice and reclamation in the face of anyone who would prefer that you don a costume and keep playing the game to maintain the status quo.

> *I will not outsource my healing to the overculture, which would prefer that I detach from my feelings; instead, I will sit with the stifled screams of my pain and give them space for true release.*

# IN FLAMES

*The same flames that scorch our tender skin*

*and burn down our houses of cards*

*are the ones that warm frozen flesh back to life*

# STANDING IN THE FLAMES

FIRE HAS BEEN A FUNDAMENTAL PART OF OUR COLLECTIVE lives for many thousands of years. It is a powerful, inherited legacy to which many of us can still feel a connection. Our ancestors cooked on fire, slept near it, and later, read by candlelight, enjoying its illuminating gifts long before electricity was discovered and harnessed.

Standing in the flames of a transformative experience can have the impact of a spiritual awakening. People who have had near-death experiences describe a light or sensations of warmth emanating from the other side. Certain heartbreaks can feel like death, and rightfully so. They are the deaths of what once was, and there is an opening for the grief that follows.

We are not a culture that welcomes grief. We are so uncomfortable with limited light sources that we have invented ways to keep lights on around us until long after dark. Giving grief its due with offerings of tears and time can find us in a place where we transition away from our "dark nights of the soul" into a lighter, inner space when the heaviness subsides. Fire is here for us in both embodiments. It sheds light and gives warmth, and it is no surprise that fire is a central part of many ceremonies of Indigenous peoples.

Fire has its own spirit that supports us in times of healing. As an ally on our journeys through the swamplands of brokenheartedness, flames dance as we gaze, holding us accountable to new visions for our lives beyond our current experience. I have had many encounters with wood fires during healing times. I have burned old cards and letters, releasing emotions into smoke as paper turns to ash. I have seen the jumping figures of animals in the flames—strange shapes and spirits encouraging me to keep going. The light cast by fire is mysterious, inconsistent, dynamic. It is not solid like rock or earth, but moving constantly. It consumes your offerings as fuel while it brightens your face.

Give your pain to the fire in prayers and watch the flames rise to change it into another form. This is the gift of fire— it transforms things into entirely other things. Your fuel of misguided beliefs, self-images, anxieties, concepts, shadows, and unresolvable conflicts are lit torches on the path to your liberation. Make time to sit with firelight and warm the parts of you that are weary and ready to let go. Healing occurs in stages, and you will have plenty of fuel to keep tending your inner fire.

 *I light the torches of liberation by offering the fuel of my outdated beliefs and patterns to the spirits in the flames.*

# WARMING THE HEART

THE HEART IS THE FIRE THAT WARMS YOU INTO ALIVENESS and helps you glow. Your heart says to your mind, "I feel your painful memories, and I'm storing them as scar tissue." Scar tissue is cool to the touch, with less blood circulating through it. We are speaking metaphorically, of course, but we know what it feels like to be hurt and have our hearts turn cold.

Wanting revenge, indulging vindictiveness, wishing bad things on people—all are signals that we've let our heart fires go cold and untended. It is part of healing to take inventory of whose head you'd like to see on a platter, but it's important not to loiter on that, as it is more poisonous to you than them. Of course, for certain crimes and abuses, there must be retribution and, without question, boundaries.

Your mind is in service to your heart, and can uplift it in a circular dialogue that empathizes with the harm you've felt. We see examples all around us of people operating from survival, from fear, from opportunism, from mean-spiritedness. When we start to train our minds to be in service to our hearts, and we tend our brokenhearted-ness and clean off its fears little by little, we begin to speak more kindly and treat ourselves with grace. This in turn prompts us to be more compassionate toward others. A warm heart is a kind heart.

None of us have been conditioned to operate from the heart; rather, we are shown by the overculture how to move from self-preservation. You can change this inner dy-namic by offering varying levels of vulnerability to intimate partnerships and friendships. You can learn to be emotion-ally safe for the loved ones you are close with. You will get to express your emotional intelligence and shed your armor with loved ones, as this is the invitation that deeper levels of relationship present.

If you are accustomed to shallower versions of relation-ships, check in with yourself about what you yearn for. What kinds of interactions help your heart stay warm? In the absence of intimate-partner relationships, look to chil-dren and friends to adore and offer safety to. You can prac-tice relational skills with anyone. Knowing what kinds of communication help you feel safe will assist you in seeking them out. Learning communication that fosters safety for others will help you build deeper relationships.

Too often, we choose partners who trigger and activate our scar tissue. This pattern is always an invitation to heal, but we are so accustomed to projecting our inner issues onto our significant others that we end up going in circles instead of standing in our heart fires together. Then, more brokenheartedness ensues. It can be especially painful if we cannot find our healing way with a partner with whom we have a strong desire to overcome our relationship struggles. We cannot take leaps of vulnerability and intimacy with one another if the painful memories of the past prevent us from feeling safe.

If you subvert your emotional intelligence by leading only with your mind, you risk becoming further disconnected from your heart. You may unconsciously overprotect. Inside relationships, you may attempt to micromanage your loved ones' feelings so you can feel safe. At its best, this behavior, rooted in anxiety, reveals vigilance with respect to demonstrating care. At its worst, it seeks to covertly control and manipulate, and doesn't allow for others' authentic experiences to unfold at a sustainable pace.

Growth takes time and perseverance, and other people's growth is ultimately not going to happen on our time and terms. When I fall toward romantic love, I develop expectations. I can become emotionally invested in caring for another in the hope that I will be cared for by them in the ways I need to be. I cut myself off from my own heart and lean into unconscious dependency. My clever mind tries to reconcile the pain of my past by overgiving love in order to receive it. We who operate like this must learn to care for our own dear hearts in a manner that opens them, become more self-contained, and cultivate healthy relationships with ourselves while healing from codependent patterns.

Deep relationships are the ones we tend to trust and value the most. We need them all around us, not just from romantic partners. We do not want love that we have to pretzel ourselves into complex forms to receive. This is manipulative, and it chokes our fire and passion. This kind of love thrives in anxious conditions that cut off circulation.

Hippocrates said, "Iron heals the diseases medicines cannot treat, and fire heals the diseases iron cannot treat; diseases that fire cannot heal are incurable." As we reignite our internal pilot light and turn our love toward ourselves, we can look to the fires of healing to burn away the dis-ease that has taken hold of our bodies and souls. In order to grow into ourselves, we must connect with the love that continues to warm our internal heart fire and create a safe haven for ourselves and others.

*I tend my heart fire, offering warmth to the parts of me that are hurting and making it safer to exchange deeper levels of care.*

# SOOTHING INFLAMMATION

WE CARRY FIXED IDEAS ABOUT HOW THINGS SHOULD BE:
Marriages should last until we're rocking on front porches
as elders, children should die after their parents, vows spoken should not be allowed to shift—so many ideas. And
yet, commitments go up in smoke. Agreements turn to
ash. Capacities burn out. The way things were is not the
way they will always be.

Anticipatory grief cannot prepare your body for wholly
felt disappointment. Termination and renegotiation, even
when desired, drip beads of sweat. We are not com-
fortable accepting the nuances of transformation, which
can be uncomfortable and awkward because it invites us
into the gnarly, liminal spaces and urges us to be patient
with ourselves before jumping immediately into the person we'll be on the other side, or crawling back into the
shell of who we were before. Accepting our movement
into new possibilities and ways of being in the world can
be painful—this kind of change can even feel like we're
betraying our former selves or past partners. The stimuli

of our new lives can be overwhelming in the same way that bright scenery filled with commotion is disturbing to a newborn baby.

The journey into an unfamiliar dimension of you-ness will find you in various bottlenecks that will shift your very bones and structures. You must soften in order to be rebirthed—willing to step into flames, be reduced to tiny ash, and emerge reformed by the fire. There will be a broad spectrum of highs and lows. Appropriate aftercare soothes inflammation. You must give this to yourself first, before seeking rescue by others or distracting yourself from your own healing by offering them support.

Heart wounds make their own medicine by rupturing the old system, creating a paste of ash and blood to draw out the infection and soothe. The heart mends itself, not with time, distraction, and forgetfulness, but with attention that does not seek to change anything. We humans tend to be fixers and solution-seekers, innovators and thinkers. Yet the heart cannot be fixed by thoughts alone. Embodying change means walking, talking, listening, and caring for yourself differently. Transformation can be painful, and you may not recognize the person who is making these new strides, but the fire of your freedom is waiting to kiss your old wounds . . . to melt you down into your primary components and rebirth you like a phoenix.

*I am willing to soften my bones to make it through the fire of my suffering, so I can get to the other side.*

# BRAVING THE CAULDRON

It takes time and practice to sit with your wounds, to be with emotional discomforts, pressures, and constrictions in your body. Some discomforts come up as fiery defenses, especially if you felt under attack growing up or in previous partnerships.

Heartache changes us in ways we do not want to be changed. The ache is part resistance to the unfoldment of events beyond our control, and part longing for what was. To cope with such complexity, some of us jump in and roll up our sleeves like medics, seeking solutions with urgency. Others buckle under stress and hide. We are not all first responders. We have not been socially trained to respond to combusting storms of confusing emotions, but our bodies know how to shut down in overwhelm and hyperperform to control situations. This is especially true if we have maladaptive coping skills that we learned in early childhood.

In the cauldron of transformation, it is not necessary to know skills you were never taught. You can facilitate soothing change by creating fresh conditions in your body that accommodate the healing process.

Early on in healing a significant heartbreak, I'm already burned out on reading, going to therapy, talking with friends. I exhaust myself by resisting the truth that something has ended, thinking I can control the outcome if I just (fill in the blank with any inauthentic adaptation). When my marriage abruptly ended, I spent the first six months in a state of complete unacceptance—a tiring tactic that felt like that popular meme where the big building is on fire and the person comes to the adjacent balcony with a small bucket of water and throws it at the inferno. I was not expecting my entire life to change on a dime, yet I still reacted in desperation in my attempt to save it, not noticing that I only needed to rescue myself from the burning building.

If I could do it over again, I envision myself roasting some marshmallows in the flames in a laughable act of surrender. Bless my heart, right? I was fastened so tightly to my wedding vows that I allowed myself to spend my already depleted reserve of energy fighting reality.

Understandably, it can be excruciating to lean into change and transform at great cost to our hopes and dreams. When our emotions are in an emergency state, catastrophe ensues. We forget that we do not have unlimited supplies of adrenaline in our bodies. We can still

express our desires and grief, while demonstrating acceptance for what we can't resuscitate . . . for what we must
willingly offer to the fires of change. Even as we watch the
flames licking the constructs of the past, charring what we
previously cherished until all of it curls in upon itself, dissolving into smoke and ash—we can slow-dance with the
nuances of our feelings.

The cauldron of transformation beckons you to put all
that you are into the brew and stir for your life. You can be
large enough to hold the sadness, bitterness, grief, and regret alongside the rising hope for what you might build to
revive the scorched earth on which you stand.

*I lean into transformation by developing*
*resources in my body that will help me surrender*
*into the fires of change.*

# BREAKING FREE OF ILLUSIONS

WHEN WE COMPLICATE THE EFFECTS OF HEARTBREAK out of fear for this stark new reality—because it contrasts with the fantasy of what could have been—it can pose blazing challenges to our vision for our life. Our resources and vision are limited, so we might choose to fight for a person or a relationship that was not generous to us, or a job that may have given us security, but was joyless or oppressive. We may look back and see a dysfunctional relationship as better than it actually was, noting its good parts instead of why it broke down. This is also true when loved ones die: We memorialize to remember the good and release everything else. This works when someone has died, for there is finality and it is honoring. We cannot bring them back. Not so with lovers.

Illusion is deceptive, especially for those of us who see the best in people and situations. When we are conditioned to fear loss, we cling to our fantasies about those people and situations—our ideas and idealizations of them, our bondage to their potential, our beholdenness to our own flawed perfectionism.

Houses of cards must inevitably burn down. It's my experience that if I do not hold a match to my illusions, life will. In flames, we allow our thoughts about who others are and what they're doing to be burned away so we can focus on our own sacred tasks. We release what others think about us. We burn our projections about what we think happened, who was right and who was wrong, what we'd do if we had another chance, what would have been if only they'd done this or that. We can hold ourselves accountable for any part we played in the breakdown, and in doing so, alight our self-blame and other-blame.

Of course, we must be discerning when it comes to recognizing that some of the people in our lives may have violated us or caused us trauma. We don't release blame to bypass our experience or avoid sitting with difficult feelings, such as betrayal or rage; we do it to release the hold that person has on us. Even in violent relationships, there can be love and care. The process of release and transformation challenges us to accept the reality of harm while acknowledging where love was present, but it need not keep dragging us back into situations that repeat toxic patterns.

If a person or a job is sucking your spirit dry, you can block their ability to influence you. Cutting ties of dependency is necessary, and this can be especially challenging if you share children with people who behave in destructive ways that harm you, themselves, and those you love.

When struggling to release what you cannot control, invest in the belief that your spirit is stronger than the desires of your ego. Don't exhaust yourself firefighting; rather, let go of whatever that person, job, or situation represents for you; release the illusion of its invincibility, or the sense that it filled you with purpose and structure that you would be bereft without. Do not be held hostage by this illusion. Security can be cultivated in relationship, but the foundation for security lies within *you*.

*I release my old illusions about the people*
*and situations that still hold my ego hostage,*
*while building foundations that give me*
*genuine security by supporting my spirit's true*
*expressions.*

# NAVIGATING REGRET

As you tend your fire on a healing path, regrets will surface. There are many events you took part in during which you betrayed or abandoned yourself or others, didn't show up with the skills to navigate wisely, and compromised your moral code. This raking of the coals is a critical part of transformative healing. It is necessary that we take inventory of how we did not honor ourselves and others; of how we didn't live up to our own integrity.

If you've ever raked coals, especially on a very cold morning after a long night, it is a gesture of salvation: piling the glowing, ash-covered chunks in the hopes of a smooth reignition. If we linger over the burned remnants too long, however, we lose the potential for renewed heat, and the spirit of the fire dies out. This is not unlike the healing process.

The phrase "raking someone over the coals" comes from the act of dragging the bodies of heretics over a bed of red-hot coals as punishment in the Middle Ages. It is an act of torture that we carry out on ourselves when we perceive that we failed to meet our own standards or those valued in the overculture.

When you are unable to repair the consequences of harmful actions, guilt and shame can add more agony to your experience. Guilt is a messenger that notifies us of wrongdoing and prompts us to do better. It can be moved through nimbly, with awareness, even when direct amends and repairs cannot be made.

Shame resides in a deeper place and points to beliefs of what bad people we are. Shame is rooted in adverse childhood experiences in which we were made to feel that our human mistakes were unforgivable. In this binary of bad and good, there is no hope for redemption. We all have our strategies to punish or numb our shame when we don't know how to reconcile it. Shame often leads us to project our wrongdoings onto others. It seeks to blame when it cannot hold the weight of having done harm. Reliving regrets in this way re-traumatizes our inner child and spirals us deeper into powerlessness.

Creating an identity from shame's accusations is poisonous to your spirit and will continue to generate unwanted consequences. The trajectory of shame, whether felt or buried, is not one that should be allowed to drive your life. Shame and its attendant unprocessed grief are responsible for many of the world's current situations. We are a culture that numbs and medicates, our heart fires having been extinguished in the process of colonizing and being colonized. Life force is diminished where shame is present. We wake up early and caffeinate to meet the demands of colonial capitalism. Who has the resources to stop and take inventory, to process generations of shame and legacy burdens that continue to replicate in our bodies? Perversely, our overculture grants "healing" primarily to those who are time- and money-rich.

Heartbreak is a blessing in disguise. It beckons us back to the campfires of our ancestors. Strong emotions that come from loss present us with the opportunity for a spiritual awakening, so that we may be reclaimed by a passion for doing life not "well," but better than we have been.

When you have stopped projecting blame onto others for what is your responsibility, it is time to address shame. Transforming the shame that finds you raking yourself over the coals sounds daunting, but it is possible. Digging into childhood to find those pivotal moments when you started to believe you were bad takes a lot of care—the kind of care loving parents give their child.

Criticism, judgment, and punishment are traditions we carry forward. If we're giving it out to others, we're also heaping it onto ourselves. Shame, like coals coated in ash, is cloaked in other emotions we were unable to express during our early development. We didn't have the language back then to stand up for ourselves and engage in clean communication like we can as adults. There is much complexity to hold as you navigate healing from childhood shame. Emotions that shroud shame include anger, rage, sadness, disappointment, and fear. Sensitivity and care are needed during what can feel like a trial by fire. The judge, jury, and executioner will need to stand down so that you can reclaim agency where it was lost.

*I acknowledge how fear and shame have stolen my life force and harmed my relationships, and I commit to gently reparenting myself.*

# TRANSFORMING THROUGH THE CONTRACTIONS

THERE IS A COMBUSTIBLE INTERNAL ENERGY THAT OCCURS when too many stressful things are happening all at once. The more fear and pressure you experience from outside influences, the more this urgency will be felt by your nervous system, and the more you will be activated to react with trauma responses of fight, flee, freeze, or appease.

Your heart feels this compression and contracts, withholding its vulnerability when in protection mode. The intense pressure to survive is like gasoline on your body, which cannot keep up with the alarming speed of technology, news, tragedy, threats, and our biggest fear: our own impending death and the demise of our species as a result of planetary neglect and extraction.

Existential guilt and grief for what has happened to our world habitat are bearing down on us each day, along with all the other fears and pressures. There are actions we can take to manage chaos, and there are many things we must surrender our will to change, because we lack any power to control them. Avoidance is one extreme, and unsustainable anxiety is the other. The middle path is in knowing when to lean toward intentional surrender and organized action. In acute stages of heartbreak, we have to surrender a lot of control so that we can rest in the process of grief and regrouping our energy. Standing with our suffering and trying to do the next right thing is not helped by swinging between extreme reactions of feeling all the feelings in a big way or cutting them off altogether.

Can you allow internal contractions and constrictions caused by pressure and pain to do their transformative work on you? Can you surrender when you don't have control and take action when you do?

Geology, under heat and pressure, eventually liquefies, leaving us with no choice but to be with the difficult truths that force us out of resistance and into decisions. This is how diamonds are made. We are humans, not diamonds, and we make mistakes. Withstanding the consequences of our actions and inactions is part of how we transform, and do the work that is required to heal. This is the process we must intrepidly undergo again and again if we choose a path of growth and maturity. Intentional entry into and surrender inside the chrysalis are how caterpillars get their wings to become butterflies.

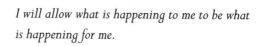

*I will allow what is happening to me to be what is happening for me.*

# RESPONDING RATHER
# THAN REACTING

When we are shaped by chaos in the family and/or the overculture, we become hypervigilant. This helps us to anticipate future attacks and keep them at bay. Our keen perception finds them even where they may not exist, because the body remembers being in chaos and reacts before we have a chance to thoughtfully respond with consideration for consequences.

You can take all of the measures to protect yourself, your family, your animals, your property. You can be six steps ahead of the game and still be held hostage by the feelings caused by past abuses and violations. The effects of being violated can be long-lasting and steal energy from your healing process. Even after I have set boundaries to protect myself, the inflammation that comes from harsh words and actions is still acutely felt. Sometimes, I still feel overprotective after I've done all I can to call in support and given myself agency to stand up for myself.

When the body and emotional systems operate on hypervigilance, new habits must be created to preserve health as we find our way to higher ground. When we become obsessed with being offended, our moods, sleep hygiene, and ability to function are impacted. Rumination on past events that cannot be changed shows up as reviewing historical material for inaccuracy and clarification, which creates flares in the body. Rumination fires us up from the inside out, keeping us stuck in a repetitive loop of misery, blame, and regret that we didn't do something differently. The parts of us that are committed to justice become collateral as we sacrifice our health to our compulsions to repeatedly visit the past and burn out our vitality.

Practice disrupting impulsive and compulsive habits of rumination on the past by putting yourself in the center of your heart as fire tender. Meditate on that fire in your heart as the fuel that will take you forward into new love, new work, new commitments, and new purpose.

*I invent new visions for the energy of my heart
and release the past over which I have no
control.*

# HEALING LEGACY BURDENS

Legacy burdens are haunting multigenerational adaptations and strategies that are passed down through conditioning, caregiver patterns, and our genetics. Extreme feelings, emotions, energies, and beliefs are transmitted through the family line, and they tend to go unquestioned and unchallenged.

The Native side of my family exhibited patterns of distrust of others, with some habits becoming more prominent as they grew older, their minds looping through past experiences and fixating on key narratives where they'd felt wronged and unreconciled. My family carries unexamined beliefs about people meddling with their finances, romantic partners betraying them, and business dealings leading to the stealing of family land without just remuneration. We even have a habit of clearing our throats and coughing repeatedly—some family members do so to the point of vomiting. Certainly, there are very real, unhealed traumas that can generate such patterns, but the patterns themselves are unviable coping mechanisms that lead to physical and mental obstacles, which we then pass down to the next generation.

Culturally speaking, when gender roles were even more prevalent than they are today, our mothers and grandmothers may have been discounted by the family system and the overculture, which led them (and us) to feeling undervalued and unheard. If our fathers and grandfathers were hardened survivalists, we may have parts of ourselves that behave in cold and hypervigilant ways, without attention to the impact we have on loved ones and the beings around us. If there is a family history of caregivers betraying or abandoning their children, members of our family could have extreme fears of being abandoned or betrayed.

Our wounds are hard to see because we've accepted through generations that this is how we are—that hardship is just the way it is. It's almost as if we have agreed to carry heavy, oversized backpacks full of our family's problems and fears, even though this was not a conscious choice.

Not all transmitted legacies are burdensome, but those that are can be healed with attention, tracking, and care. All of us have these wounds, which we become more aware of as we gain more experience within relationships outside of our family system. While they may be significant parts of our personality, we can choose to transform the burdens that are creating issues for us.

Part of healing legacy burdens is to declare that you do not consent to carry destructive traditions forward. If you adopted a fear of people stealing from you, and it's causing you to feel possessive or covetous, preventing you from sharing your love or resources, consider that protectiveness is a good thing—but not in extremes. One extreme I experience is feeling my blood boil when I witness people using spiritual vocations to manipulate followers for the purpose of satisfying their ego, or to obtain sex or money. If I perceive cultishness, it causes extreme reactions of fierce protectiveness in me. There is nothing wrong with fierce protectiveness, except when it becomes a disproportionate response to the situation at hand. I've had to study how my extremes seem more conditioned within me than my childhood experiences warrant. Overprotectiveness pushes loved ones away. Consider that ingredients such as these can create inflammatory conditions in your body when held tightly or poorly channeled.

When you sense that you are disconnected or dissociated from your body, or experiencing extreme states of emotion, explore the heartbreak in your family stories. There is no redemption in continuing to suffer for the harms your ancestors endured. It is not a gift to them. They already lived through such experiences, and you don't need to relive them in a misguided form of honoring. There are many ways to recognize the injustice of the past and what your ancestors endured while liberating your body from the ongoing felt sense of their distress and annihilation. Activists, justice workers, and people in helping professions have found ways to channel the compassionate generosity that was missing from their ancestors' lives. Bringing meaning and purpose to what lights you up is time well spent.

*I take responsibility for the legacy burdens*
*that live in me by trading suffering for applied*
*action.*

# RE-ATTUNING TO OUR
# INNER LANDSCAPE

We are in constant anxiety about what is happening to our habitat. I see this in my teenage children in the form of deep concern about whether there will be a world for them to finish growing up in. Since they were little, they have been aware of what is now being called "climate justice." I once heard them refer to their weariness as "eco-fatigue," and all of my bells rang. Worrying about the state of our habitat puts us in states of hyperarousal and fatigues us in the extreme.

Our relationships are ecosystems, too, dependent on nutrients that we feed them like sacred offerings to keep them thriving. When, like a root-bound plant, we fail to provide spaciousness and new soil, love can become constricted. It cannot breathe. It begins to slowly turn on itself until we can no longer discern between the damage we fear and the damage we are doing.

Yes, it is anxiety-inducing to feel our planet warming, to visually witness the burn of our suffering ecosystems—

forests dry up because trees are infested with beetles, plastic piles up in mountains on the ocean floor, thick blankets of smog hang over cities, and wildlife species are disappearing. It is excruciating to straddle two truths: that we humans are burning down our own houses, and that Earth is responding in kind to this destruction. What is most concerning is our inability to agree upon, and prioritize, actionable repairs to ensure we will have livable habitats for several more generations.

We are out of touch with our primary purpose of preserving life on Earth for future generations. We must re-attune ourselves to our inner ecosystems if we are to provide nourishment and stewardship for our outer ecosystems. But processing deep levels of neglect of the self and the world is impossible to do in one sitting. It requires patience and compassion for ourselves, as well as the mistakes and missteps we will inevitably make along the way to healing ourselves and the planet.

None of it is easy or straightforward. In the places where I have experienced neglect in my personal life, nerves, when touched, are like hot wires prodding tender knobs of flesh. Acknowledging my capacity for neglect—of my children when I'm too busy to check in or notice their needs, of my home, of friendships that have grown apart, of failed relationships I haven't been willing to admit my part in—is too shameful and overwhelming to face. Staying on this track while scapegoating others digs me into a deep rut that is difficult to get out of. This is another way that shame causes us to shrink our potential through avoidance. Our habitat, our mother and provider of all needs, is being impacted by our neglect; without her thriving health, this means we, too, will continue to neglect our own children.

Many times, I have felt the double whammy of shame and powerlessness to change these destructive patterns. I remind myself: As within, so without. If I cannot change my inner practices of self-destruction and neglect, I will truly be powerless to do my part to shape a world that many more generations can enjoy.

The work will always be here for us, and we must approach it with clarity and compassion. We are here to do our inner reconciliation and generate compassionate fire to show up in different ways.

*I commit to heal from the self-neglect that comes from heartbreak, and to make repairs to my inner and outer landscapes.*

# ENERGETICALLY MENDING
# THE SACRED ALTAR

Courage is a foundation that is forged in the midst of loneliness and self-reflection, and it finds new bits of inspiration and building materials along the journey. Creativity accompanies this courage, a gift of reconnecting to your heart. I'm experiencing it right now as I write these words to you.

Believe me when I tell you that writing a book while living through the heartache of shattered dreams has come with many cold nights when I was too damn tired to tend my fire. Plagued by shock, abandonment, lack of appetite, a cancer scare, adrenal fatigue, single parenting (again!), humiliation, isolation, COVID, overgiving, and overworking—how on earth can one expect to find creative inspiration in such states of emotional, mental, and physical overwhelm?

I kept a journal to track myself because I was experiencing problems with my memory and motor skills. Some heartbreaks are so deep, they fracture our abilities to function. Very slowly, when the more dramatic and engulfing feelings began to metabolize, a close friend would remark, "Today you have fire in your face!" These were rare days when I showered and got a little bit of sleep. I was living betwixt and between the worlds of the living and the dead, and so a day of fire in my face meant I was more on the living side, which was helpful to remember.

There would be moments of overwhelming grace and gratitude, and in these winks, I could feel a profound love, greater than what I had lost, nudging me to doodle with a pencil on binder paper, write a deliciously dreary poem, dance to a wild song, or make myself a meal other than cold cereal and milk. I cherished these moments of creative inspiration, even when they were just a quick whisper. I wrote them in my journal so that I would remember I am my own autonomous being with my very own relationship to the spirits, who are guiding me and teaching me about life through how I cope with loss.

I am thankful that the body is creative by design. Humans are generative beings who make, solve, and repair anew. After disaster strikes, we fix our roofs and rebuild our cities, we get new ideas to create better systems and structures, we arrange flowers for pleasure, and we plant gardens that do more for our spirits than feed our bellies.

Our tissues mend when torn, and our bones heal when broken—and so can we mend our hearts.

Your heart is the central hub, the engine of your passionate being. When it is injured or in the process of massaging scar tissue and proud flesh back into sensitization, the motor is working overtime. Healing takes energy and resources, and the healing process can remove your attention from other people, places, and things that you value.

If your car engine had an unfixable crack, you would need to replace it. This is not an option when it comes to our heart—most of us will take the heart we were born with to our graves. While we cannot replace the architecture of our being, we can choose to energetically mend what has been rent asunder or emotionally demolished.

Energetic mending of your sacred altar is up to you. When your heart receives mending, your creative energy gets a boost. When you have energy for passion projects and giving generously to yourself and others, you will know you're coming back to your heart. The heat that inflames us also infuses our creativity, animating it and fleshing it into form.

In ceremonies around the world, a fire often sits at the center of a circle, symbolizing the energy we came into the world with, and our hearts that sparked us into life not long after conception. The heart likes to be warmed. The warmer it is, the more blood it pumps to our bodies. Circulation is optimal when we warm our hearts, and love pours easily and effortlessly, almost as if we were sitting by a fireplace and soaking in the comforting heat.

*May the radiance of my soul come through the creative expressions and energetic mending of my heart.*

# DANCING IN THE INFERNO

WHEN WE ARE DEEP WITHIN HEARTACHE, WE ARE DANC-ING in a partnership with our child self, with our hurt adult self, with the pain that happened in adulthood awaking the childhood pain, and with intergenerational pain itself. It's a big undertaking to get on your knees and ask this pain to heal you. It is at times a tiresome strain to connect to and listen for what you need that you must give yourself—that only *you* can give yourself.

While heartbreak isn't unique, your process is deeply personal, layered, and complex. Competing inner dialogues can become frustrating when the pain is dull and unrelenting. Heartbreak is not a clinical condition but the depression that accompanies it can cloud the joys you want to experience.

If your senses desire a lift, remember that fire reunites you with what is ancient and eternal within you—and what you smell, touch, taste, see, and hear colors your day. When I'm grieving, it helps me to stay close to prayer and to fire as much as possible. I build many fires with wood, and with that, I build my relationship to fire itself.

As an elemental, fire has been speaking to its tenders for thousands of years. You can ask it to tell you stories and secrets. In many Indigenous traditions, fire is an archetype and a personality. It helps with purification, cleansing, testing of one's will, and burning away energetic detritus.

There are many ways to connect with the purifying fire that has raged and lulled us with its graceful flames through the ages. You can build a literal fire and ask it to tell you its secrets, to reunite you with what is ancient and tender and formidable within you. You can eat spicy food that reconnects you to passion and sensation. You can bask in the sun (without getting burned) and let the light rays beam down on you, reminding you of that which gives life. You can stoke your own internal, sacred fire by having sex with yourself if you feel like a safe partner.

My trial by fire took me through many changes of my own. I got several meaningful tattoos and adopted a kitty. (I practically lived at the local cat shelter; each precious feline holds its own unique and unquenchable fire.) I read *Undrowned* by Alexis Pauline Gumbs and *Everything Is Fucked* by Mark Manson. I started a twelve-step program. I sat in Native ceremonies with fire at the center. I grew *tanchi*, *tohbi*, and *isito* (corn, beans, and squash) for my tribal nation. I leaned into friends who were also experiencing heartbreak. I practiced new forms of reverence and irreverence. I made a raunchy dance playlist. I let my tears flow unabated. I listened to my own heart beating. I trusted the energy to move, and I did all I could to create favorable conditions inside myself for movement. Mobilization was critical.

Accordingly, the fire within you can be fed in so many ways. Make art. Dance. Let your body move you. See theater, music, film. Read poetry—there is a hidden language in verse that is waiting for you to decode it. Cultivate faith in a power greater than yourself and surrender to it. Light a candle and summon your ancestors. Place your hands on your heart and feel for the sacred drumbeat, which sparked to life within weeks of your conception. Follow your heart—its flame may feel dim or faint, but trust that it has always been here, waiting for you to feed it, and waiting to feed you in turn.

*When I'm feeling dull and lifeless, I connect to my heart fire and imagination by building relationships with the world around me, including nonhuman helpers.*

# UNDER WATER

*We contain in these bodies*

*the lubricating substance*

*that gives life*

*that covers most of Earth*

*It is ours to drown in*

*or be hydrated by*

*as is our will*

# EBBING AND FLOWING

Making kinship with water is life-affirming. Water unburdens us from gravity when we spend time with it. It cleanses our skin and hydrates us, purifying our blood and helping our vital organs do their jobs to keep our bodies healthy. The emotional landscape is represented by water, just like Earth's surface and depth. All of Earth's fate is determined by what water is doing—where it's rising, evaporating, freezing, and precipitating. These changes, even when subtle, affect all plants and animals, including humans.

In our relationship with our emotions, we can be fluid, ever-changing, but with some predictable patterns based on our personal histories. Feelings ebb and flow, and they also drive our passions and our decisions. We can track where we have made feelings-based decisions throughout our lives and note where our emotions were in reliable communication with our thoughts and choices. In this way, we learn to develop kinship with our inner waters, and we can go so far as to cultivate respect for the emotions that seem to be mostly in charge of our lives. I hear from people who are afraid to have a conscious relationship with their real or deeper feelings; they fear that doing so might create a cascading waterfall of problems and overwhelm them.

Feelings are not the single most important aspect of our lives, but considering them is tantamount to honoring them. Just as water is not the single most important aspect of our body's health, it's true that we cannot go without it. Some feelings, like rage, have had to remain closeted so as not to come bursting out, causing big discomfort. However, rage must have a place to be expressed if it is living inside us. It is a sacred and appropriate response to injustice, but when misdirected, rage causes unwanted problems with other people we are in a relationship with. While depression is considered a state of being, it isn't an emotion. When we feel depressed—and I believe most of us have some experience with feeling this way—emotions are pushed down and may feel too confusing and nebulous to manage. It can feel like being underwater or "in over our heads." We concern ourselves much more with what is causing these low-grade states that feel disabling but are not classified as a disability.

It is very challenging to allow ourselves to feel and accept the discomfort of depression. For me, it feels dorsal, like sitting very quietly at the bottom of the ocean. I have trouble mobilizing or moving my thoughts in a direction that's more supportive of my overall health.

Heavy clouds in the emotional forecast call for us to appreciate the nourishing waters they will bring, but we don't prefer the "gloomy" days. Here, we find ourselves caught in another binary with our biases, in which we believe "up" and "sunny" is a better way to be. "Up" is associated with fewer limits, I suppose. Sometimes, the desire to transform "down" to "up" comes from cultural forces that are uncomfortable with the stillness associated with depressive states. It is hard to be with myself when I don't feel mobile. The overculture is very concerned with mobility. We must always be producing to feel okay about ourselves. This is life in a meritocracy, where our worth is based on what we get done.

In my second half of life, I am becoming perfectly all right with not participating in this way of being. Instead, I honor my waters. You can honor the ebb and flow of your emotional waters in real time by floating, weeping, swimming, surfing, bathing, or steaming. You can be with your changing moods and not expect them to be different from what they are. You can observe the many shapes of water and see that your body is like Earth, who expresses her waters in infinite ways.

*I honor water when I value myself in my ebb and flow, regardless of how productively I express myself.*

# CRYING AS CLEANSING

TEARS CLEANSE OUR EMOTIONAL BODIES OF PAIN AND grief, but sometimes we don't allow them to flow. Depending on the messaging we received as children, whether we were embraced and encouraged to have our feelings or were forced to shut down our emotional bodies, determines how we form our ideas and behaviors around crying.

Crying is a display of vulnerability, but it has been accused of being weaponized as a tool of manipulation, as well. We carry resistance, and sometimes shame, toward our tears. People often apologize for crying. We quickly offer tissues to stop the flow.

When I have gathered circles of individuals to share their experiences and practice communally held healing, tears tend to be abundant. There are not many safe spaces where we can tell our stories and where our pain can be held. When we get to sit in such spaces, we can come loaded with emotions we've been hiding behind a dam for years. When the dam breaks, it can feel overwhelming.

Waters are healthy when they are in motion. When dammed, they can become stagnant, layered with experiences new and old. We use language to describe when something "moves us," which indicates that emotions are being stirred. Imagine a pool with sediment at the bottom. When circulated, the sediment rises to the top and swirls with the water. This can feel like a murky and messy process, but it's integral to the healing.

If our tears surprise us, they are an indicator that something wants to be expressed. Allowing expression feels vulnerable and triggers fear about whether we will be accepted in such a state. Our feelings are not dirty, by any means. Like the clothes we wear that pick up dust and detritus from the living world around us and from our bodies that they lie against, we clean our garments without questioning why. Our bodies are cleansed through honest expression, and tears move feelings up and out. A good cry can leave us feeling healed or emptied of what we've been holding inside.

As we make more room for tears, ours and those of others, we resensitize ourselves with new cultural values that allow for the regular cleansing of our emotional bodies and create a path for healing to be part of our daily lives. Weeping is part of how we express joy and pain. People who discourage weeping have not accepted that this natural flow of emotion is part of how we release and maintain healthy emotional hygiene. Even if we have been conditioned to hold back, we are fortunate to have much visual and auditory media with the power to touch our hearts and, like tides and currents, move our feelings around until we are alive with the flow.

*I challenge cultural norms that discourage tears,*
*and I weep as I feel called, without apology.*

# GETTING LOST IN LIQUID

THOSE WHO ARE BROKENHEARTED AND DO NOT HEAL often end up breaking other hearts.

Growing up in an alcoholic, codependent home, I developed many judgments about alcoholism and addiction. I believed that people who used didn't care about their families, that addicts are narcissists and sociopaths, that alcoholics are weak and choose to numb out rather than stand up and face their pain. I refused to share anyone with their demons. I saw people abstaining from alcohol and narcotics as safer and more emotionally available to understand *me,* because I'd been a victim of behaviors like theirs. Maybe if they treated me well enough and followed all my rules, they could get some redemption.

Likewise, we tend to create positive projections that leave out the nuance and self-reflection needed to face our own anxieties and discomforts. I did not comprehend that I would need to do that for myself. I ran in the other direction, away from substance abuse and toward my pain and grief, vowing to sweep nothing under the rug. My harsh judgments helped me avoid what had hurt me so much. What I couldn't see was that reliance on others to behave and make choices so I could feel safe was its own kind of addiction, and it depended heavily on me controlling environments, people, places, and things for me to feel safe and secure in my relationships.

In *The Smell of Rain on Dust: Grief and Praise*, Martín Prechtel refers to people who have been pulled under by the waves of grief and turned to drinking as being "lost in liquid." He is referring to becoming lost in the bottle. Prechtel speaks of those experiencing addiction as requiring levels of compassion and care that I had not cultivated. My judgment was getting in the way. I wanted to cut addicts and their drama out of my life, and I didn't understand the ways in which this action kept the cycles going. Being across from addiction meant I was the victim of their behaviors. I wanted, in my codependence, for my partners to center me and my experiences.

When I looked deeper, I realized that what I really wanted was for my partners to center and protect me from harm. I wanted my rage at not being adequately cared for to find a soft landing in my primary relationship. I wanted compassion and empathy. When people experiencing addiction and its effects cannot contend with their grief, those of us across the table get to negotiate boundaries and limits. If we cannot be a helpful person in their grief process because we are too young, or we personally feel the impact, someone else will have to sit with them, listen to them, and put the washcloth on their foreheads. We have to accept their limitations and ours.

Expectations of ourselves and others are often based on ideal circumstances and fantasies. But like the great ocean, there are unpredictabilities with active addiction and sobriety/recovery that cause too much anxiety, insecurity, and stress to manage. We cannot be a life raft for cherished people, even when we would very much like to be their saviors and moral conscience. We can pray for them, sing their names, appreciate their good parts, and remember that no one truly wants to be "lost in liquid."

There are daily battles at sea taking place among people carrying heavy cargo loads of ungrieved pain and low self-worth, made complex by the coping mechanisms that continue to harm, which create more shame. You cannot comprehend what life is like inside others if you've not experienced it yourself. If I have not stood on the deck daily under thrashing sails, to sword fight my worth and will to live, I can only listen. It is not okay for me to expect from, or judge, those who struggle this way. I do not have to partner up with people who suffer certain struggles if it is too much for me. This is what heartbreak teaches.

*I do not poison myself with judgment about what I do not have experience with.*

THE WOUND MAKES THE MEDICINE

# SINKING OR SWIMMING

In the innermost life—the parts of our existence that we experience without another witness aside from the inner "I" (or the inner eye)—there are sensations of loneliness and memories that cause us to wonder whether there is a place for us. After all, there are people who have left us lonely and wanting, hungry and afraid.

Do you feel like you belong to something greater than the sum of your life's experiences? Can you learn to love your loneliness? The task is to refrain from taking pity on yourself. Pity is often confused for love. We think that sentiments of "poor me—see how I've suffered!" acknowledge the pain we've lived through, but they only serve to drown us in the overwhelm of that secret place into which we've been submerged. Secret places are desolate lake bottoms. We sink into its depths; we struggle, we rage, and we wallow in soggy mud with alarming little unwanted things tickling our ankles. Make no mistake: This is not loving our loneliness but isolating with our compulsions. Loving our loneliness, our emptiness, is looking to the horizon without expectation, unpossessed by narrative of suffering and addiction.

Feelings of loneliness prompt fixes, and it is okay to remedy aloneness by reaching out to someone who helps you feel less alone. Feeling alone is different from believing you are all alone or thinking you will always be alone. Believing and thinking turn secret desolate places of isolation into poisonous wells full of many slimy creatures who seek to swallow you up and keep you down. Feelings lead to thoughts, and thoughts lead to beliefs. It is a steep drop-off to allow feelings to turn into dangerous zones. It is important to let feelings just be feelings: transient, fluid, passing. Can you swim these sometimes-treacherous waters without drowning? Can you treasure all that you find and feel—including the numb parts, the dead parts, including what surfaces from the murky floor when you feel bleak and unaccompanied?

Try to experience the sensation of the words on your lips, trembling in response to the tender ache, to the tiny voice that asks if you can love all parts of you. There is especially a part of you that struggles to stay afloat amid the loss and betrayal; its eyes are bright and hungry, clothing ragged and nearly threadbare. It's hard to look at this part of you; it's hard to accept.

You may not like the abandoned part of you—the part that struggles with solitude, that paces, putters, and distracts. And how could this be otherwise? Our loneliness is one of the most rejected and least soothed parts of us—because we have an intrinsic belief that we are *meant* to belong. And it's true that we are collective beings, who are *meant* to belong together, to and with others—but there is another truth that dances with this one: We are also *meant* to feel and honor our emptiness. This is because there are times when we must learn to be our own best company. This is what teaches us to swim in the cold, storm-tossed regions of our lives—meaning this is what enables us to accompany our own grief, and it will help us to be genuine company in the presence of others when it is time to be together.

The anxiety of loneliness finds us seeking a well from which to drink. It is not easy to stay on the raft in the middle of the ocean, no land or other creatures in sight. So, maybe you are seeking the One who will accompany you through life's storms.

The wound of unchosen isolation runs much deeper than the wells of the people from which we drink—the latter runs out, and the former is never in short supply. Loneliness makes its own medicine when you come to accept that there is nothing wrong with you. There is nothing to fix or remedy. All you need to do is be with your own body: Sit still and quiet until you can hear your heartbeat moving your lifeblood—that river that flows into the ocean—along your internal tributaries, sustaining you. Companioning yourself, being with yourself when you don't prefer to be, is an invitation to soothe the ancient pieces of your heart that have had to endure the pain of loneliness and the bereftness of conversation or touch.

What if the well you are so thirsty for is clear and present, and it can be filled with the acceptance of your own scarred and sacred heart? In this way, loneliness is transmuted and becomes a life-giving elixir. You come to see that feelings, which seemed definite just a moment ago, are transient and not fixed. They are like clouds, pregnant with water and bursting in the skies overhead; they come and they go. They fill us with misery from time to time, and they also water the Earth.

Today, you are hit by the gravity of your loneliness. Tonight, you may feel the comfort of the cosmic mystery all around you. Tomorrow, you may share a smile with a passerby that feels connective and uplifts you in the moment. How you perceive and think about loneliness will determine the ease with which you can sit and be with it. Your beliefs about protecting your emptiness will be supportive.

*I belong with others and I belong in my loneliness—I belong in all ways.*

# STILLING OUR SYSTEM

TRAUMA IS DESCRIBED AS TOO MUCH HAPPENING TOO fast for the nervous system to metabolize. Each of us has different levels of tolerance for events, differences in how we perceive adverse experiences, and varying levels of emotional confusion based on our early development. When we do not feel safe, especially when we *should* feel safe, violations cause bewilderment.

When my traumas are triggered—especially when I'm navigating heartbreak—I experience brain fog and adrenaline surges wherein my whole body feels activated. Motor skills start to sputter. A torrent of unexpected emotions and sensations overcomes an activated body, which makes unconscious and sometimes rapid decisions to freeze, appease, flee, or fight. Hopelessness is a disheartening effect of experiencing frequent triggers within relationships.

If we think of our emotions as bodies of water—smooth and glassy when things are going well, and choppy and stormy when agitated—hopelessness might be a small, stagnant pond in which sorrows sit untended. Creating movement from this place is difficult. When the gloom of heartbreak is compounded by activated traumas, we can find ourselves in desperate states.

What has helped me most is not judging my hopelessness. When we can accept that emotional states are transient, this can create conditions for surrender and eventual mobilization. Lingering in small, dank ponds is not where we feel we can afford to hang out for too long.

I have a child who experiences frequent hopelessness. This child expects so much of the self, and this creates pressure to do something at a time when there is little energy for doing. Trusting the process is part of what helps. Explaining this to an angsty teenager—or the angsty teenager within—is often a losing battle. However, I think of the quiet, still-pond state as necessary for healing. If we do not know hopelessness, how will we know hope?

Being still requires patience with our humanness, which we are still figuring out how to allow. Fear of sinking too low beyond the point of no return is real. If I imagine my body as a cool, still, immobilized pool, can I gently look around from that state and let my vision take in the landscape? I'm asking my mind, which is scared, to connect with my heart, which is sad. I can attune to how my own sadness scares me. We are frightened of how sad we can sometimes feel. When we aren't able to distract from or control how sad we feel, the only option is to be with it.

We can bear more water than we believe we can. We can still our systems by allowing and giving grace to how afraid we are of how we feel.

*I acknowledge that I can feel very sad without needing to direct or control it.*

# FALLING INTO THE RIVER

When I was an infant, I fell into the Mighty Kern River, which runs west out of the Tehachapi Mountains down through my hometown of Bakersfield, California. Many Irish/Choctaw families migrated from Southeastern Oklahoma into the Central Valley for farming opportunities after the Indian Relocation Act was passed in 1956 to encourage Natives to move off reservations for vocational training and to achieve the next level of assimilation.

The Kern River isn't known for its tasty black bass or fifteen kinds of pepper-speckled trout, or even its Class 5 rapids that draw visitors for river rafting. The Kern is most famous for being the deadliest river in the United States. I don't have a memory of falling off the grassy bank into the river in my first spring on Earth, but my young parents looked up from their picnic, and I was gone. My mother jumped in to save me from the Killer Kern, and the event has always felt significant to my life. I imagine what it was like being underwater again, as I'd been in my mother's womb. Did I panic? Soften? Surrender my little dimpled limbs to the flow? I was a baby, and I needed a quick rescue from the waters that could claim my life, even as they'd once sustained me.

I've always felt a bit panicky in deep water for too long. I wonder if my body remembers that it needed someone else to do what I couldn't do for myself. Grief feels this way to me. I do not yield easily to it, even after decades of practice. My first instinct is always to fight to get to the surface. My mind fixates on sense-making, I hold my breath, my body spends adrenaline I can't afford, and my sleep hygiene and appetite become unreliable. I try to control my emotions that frighten me. I'm still learning how to surrender to waters that feel threatening, but I'm learning that I float easily when I let go and trust that I'm here for myself and every undertow of emotions. In this way, you too can learn to find regulation when you fall into the proverbial river.

 *I release my panic and allow myself the gift*
*that comes from navigating sometimes-turbulent*
*waters.*

# WADING INTO THE DEEP END

FIGHTING WITH MY CHILDREN IS MY CLUE THAT I'M wading into the deep end, where my healing attention is most needed. During these times of nitpicking—making mountains out of molehills, wanting them to have more respect and integrity than they're showing up with, expecting them to remember details, be on time, be organized—it feels like I'm fighting with my inner child in the same ways I was conditioned as a youth. I am repeating the patterns of my childhood and projecting my needs and anxieties onto my kids.

When I'm fighting with my partner, it seems to me that I'm really fighting with my parent. It's not about the dishes; it's about disconnection. So, in essence, we are fighting for connection. Attachment theory teaches us that the way we attached to early caregivers and the ways they handled us strongly influence the struggles in our closest relationships. If our parents were not attuned to us, meaning they misunderstood our needs, we may feel confused about how a relationship is supposed to work.

An example is when a child is terrified of a loud noise and runs to the parent in an emotional state, and the parent says, "Don't be afraid," thereby rejecting the child's feelings by pushing them away or turning energy and attention off in time of need. During development, this misguided parenting strategy sets the child up for emotional confusion. It invalidates and misdirects the child's feelings, and the child begins to patch an emotional system together, no matter how harmful it is, so the child can be acceptable to the parents. A child may learn to push down the message of fear in order to appear "tough," or to ignore the signs of activation and the need for tender attunement and regulation.

Our minds are working overtime at too young an age to figure out how all of this is supposed to work, so our adaptive brains start changing up the wiring until our feelings, actions, and facial expressions get the right response: love and care. And sometimes, this response never comes.

My children and my partner are my "grace projects," and so am I. When I give love and care to my closest loved ones who have the most power over my emotions, I am practicing how to give love and care to myself. When I attune rather than defend, my emotional system receives a healing and our relationship is prioritized over the traumas that cause maladaptive responses.

Love, and our strong need for it, is much scarier than hate, which is why it often comes with embattled words and grievances. To give and receive love is vulnerable, because we engage in love with the desire to experience it, and the belief that perhaps we won't. We mistake the beauty of our solitude—when we have the opportunity to reflect on our wants and needs—for loneliness, which we try to avoid at all costs, even if that means seeking out miserable company. But in truth, even in the moments when we feel alone and lost, we are always connected on some level, although this isn't necessarily obvious.

Nothing that comes to you is by your doing alone. We are a result of the choices we have made, including the capacities and limitations of our brain and body, as well as the conditioning we received from our caregivers and society itself. There is no self-made person. Self is a fabricated idea predicated on the knowledge and subsequent feelings that come from our experiences as separate "selves."

We tread a fine line between taking credit for our perceived successes and yielding to a knowing that we are part of a web of many fates and many selves coming together to create ever-changing results. What lives in you as pain and suffering can be transformed into delight for the body you animate, while the repetitive and mundane aspects of life—often encompassed in our relationships—comprise the container that shapes us, like a vessel holding water.

*I energize my life when I enjoy the process of communal and assisted transformation.*

# NURTURING THE FEMININE
# IN US ALL

IN THIS ERA, ALL OF US ARE LEARNING ABOUT THE HARM caused by thinking solely in binaries. In the case of jump-starting your car battery or electrical wiring, it's important to know that there is a positive and a negative charge to work with: conduits that send and receive flow.

You are probably familiar with the wounded masculine and the wounded feminine aspects that live in all genders. We crown ourselves as kings and queens in order to cultivate high regard for ourselves, especially when we've overcome an ordeal we didn't know how we'd make it through—but it's important for us to also come to terms with the shadow aspects of these two polarities that have presided over the human imagination for such a long time.

The qualities of the feminine have long been associated with water, in our long-held remembrances of women gathering at the river's edge, in the amniotic fluid that bathes and nourishes embryos, in the suit of cups in the tarot. I've come to think of these aspects as the parts of us that flow and change, let go and receive. The feminine qualities that move through each of us are gestures of ambiguity, fluidity, and receptivity.

Historically, childbearing people were thought to be endowed with a mystical, life-giving power. Menstruation and childbirth were sacred prehistoric rites, and those who endured them and found their strength were exalted and sometimes feared. Femininity has been reenvisioned as something that all of us contain and that is available to us, regardless of sex or gender; the same is true for masculinity. We each have the option to wear these qualities within and on our bodies as an expression of our wholeness.

However, all of us must come to terms with the ways in which femininity and masculinity have been wounded; and our understanding of each of these archetypes tainted. In particular, there is a great wounding of the feminine that has taken place under patriarchy; females and those expressing feminine qualities have been relegated to second-class citizens who experience more frequent instances of violence than those with masculine-dominant expressions. The darker their skin, the more violence they will experience. The poorer they are, the more violence they are likely to endure. Mounting pressures can lead to making more patriarchal bargains to nurture partners and children, while holding the shadows of the wounded masculine in exchange for room and board.

Femininity is perceived as seductive and wily, and also as weak. This has created disastrous consequences for all of us. There is a stigma associated with the feminine—and the wisdom and beauty of the feminine have been negated and degraded. This is limiting and hurts everyone. It is time for the healing waters of the feminine to wash over all of us and restore us to wholeness.

*I embrace my feminine qualities of softness and receptivity, growing ever more willing to expand my consciousness into a liberating spectrum of expressions.*

# HEALING FROM PATRIARCHY

As a survivor of patriarchy, I will always be examining the ways in which I internalized self-oppression, raised in a culture that oppresses women and still holds us as second-class citizens. I will forever be holding my inner masculinity accountable for how it acts out in learned, oppressive ways: to my children, in business, in my relationships with romantic partners.

The overculture of hypermasculinity asks me to disconnect; to discount the watery, mutable, infinitely wise domain of my intuition; to leave my body; to dismiss justice in exchange for the benefits it provides me, including a false sense of security. I use my internalized male superiority as a way to protect myself from predators. It has taught me to self-sabotage and self-betray. I learned to put expectations for money and its attaboys and rewards before my family, my relationships, and the Earth. I uphold disaster capitalism each day I live under its rule.

When I meditate on what overidentification with patriarchal masculinity feels like in my body, I am anxious.

There is a felt sense that I am up to my chest in murky water I cannot see into. I am afraid as I experience self-oppression; in fact, the water feels heavy and constricting.

We all are survivors of patriarchy who internalize its father-centric rigidity and project it onto ourselves and others in harmful ways—through force, coercion, extraction, the myth of progress, and power over rather than power with. While living in the middle of a regime that is thousands of years old, how do we counter it?

The wound of oppressive culture inside me makes medicine by defining new values that reject binary-determined authority. The process of queering—that is, releasing bias and attachments to binaries that appease patriarchal standards—is alchemy we conduct on the inside. It does not have to do with whom or how we prefer to have sex. Medicine for one extreme is not derived by swinging to the opposite extreme. We find balance when we undulate gently in the middle of the ocean, with loyalty to no extremes—only to our own wholeness.

*I reject being used as a tool for extremism's benefit; I seek and find my own wholeness.*

# MOVING AGAINST THE TIDES
# OF THE OVERCULTURE

THE WATERS WE ARE COLLECTIVELY SWIMMING IN
today threaten to drown us all. Patriarchy's violent domi-
nance imprisons and objectifies, while capitalism's demands
on our bodies encourage pursuits of status and ego through
meritocracy and diminish our health and the health of our
habitat. Governing systems poison the water we drink and
wash in, that nourish our freshwater and saltwater relatives
and food sources. Our government is Walmart, Amazon,
Apple, Facebook/Meta, big oil, and big pharma—not the
two dysfunctional, battling parents in red and blue that we
get excited about every four years.

Living within the whirlpools that keep us anxious and
productive is impacting our health and our relationships to
one another, and to the Earth that provides for us. Some
Native peoples and their allies act as Water Protectors who
set boundaries to remove hydroelectric dams and prevent
oil transport through rivers and waterways that impact
tribes.

The Standing Rock Sioux Tribe received media coverage starting in 2016, when they organized against Energy Transfer Partners to oppose the Dakota Access pipeline, an oil conduit that carries up to 750,000 gallons of crude oil per day through a section of the Missouri River as Lake Oahe. Pipeline spills impact the water of tens of millions of people and countless ecosystems. The waters we are swimming in are the ones in which deregulated businesses can operate without federal permissions and adequate environmental investigations. Battles for water are taking place all over the United States at sites of dams, fracking, and pipelines. Battles to protect water are wars between enormous businesses and the people.

The waters we're swimming in are the ones in which the basic needs of the people are neither heard nor met. As you heal from the effects of personal heartache, remember that we are collectively experiencing heartbreak from having to close our hearts and keep from feeling the intense pain of destruction to humanity and Earth's life-giving waters. As without, so within. As the waters are extracted from, exploited, devalued, and defiled, so are our spirits and our access to life-giving resources.

*I conjure energy with the collective to swim against the tides that threaten me and all my relatives.*

# ENTERING THE CURRENT TOGETHER

ALL OF OUR ANCESTORS LIVED NEAR WATER SOURCES. Rivers, creeks, and oceans provide hydration, a wide variety of seasonal food, wild game that comes to drink, reeds and grasses, and ways to cleanse. Water, like Earth, has been an abundant producer of livelihood since the dawn of humankind.

I often imagine a great many of us choosing to honor the waters that flow through and cleanse our hearts, even when they are breaking or broken by past events. It is a courageous choice to move the culture along in an evolved way that encourages resiliency but is not entangled in the fierce independence we've been conditioned with. We are moving on from inauthentic lone-wolf states that seem to insulate us from further pain while actually causing us even more pain. People belong with people, and we are learning again how to be with one another.

In my vision, I see an immense river, like the Bokchito, which my ancestors swam across to get into Indian Territory from what would later be called Mississippi and

Alabama. *Bok* means "river," and *chito* means "large." These experiences of rivers in my living memory represent the big flow of emotions that we stand in when in the throes of heartache.

There is immense beauty in imagining that through these ordeals, I am becoming more sovereign—and yet I am not alone. It's as if I can feel the water up to my chest and see another relative just upstream carrying out the same sacred task of being with their feelings. We comrades are sprinkled all up and down this river.

I'm hearing more and more talk about taking time to be with our feelings of grief and loss. And yet, we need not rescue each other. This is interdependence: the system of connectedness. It is the ease of knowing you are here with me, that we recognize each other here, and that you cannot do my sacred inner work for me. We can stand in the current of healing together as witnesses while trusting one another with our own unique processes. Healing our hearts from ordeals builds relationships. When we share how we are moving through the rivers of grief and not around them, we cultivate a special kinship that can help without trying to rescue or fix another.

*I am comforted by the presence of others around me in the current, without the need for rescue.*

# BIRTHING THROUGH
# THE SACRED PORTAL

HEARTBREAK IS BY ALL ACCOUNTS AN INITIATION. WHAT we learn from being in the deep waters of grief and loss brings us through a sacred portal. Not unlike your birth, when you passed with your embryonic, saline waters from your carrier's vessel into the world, heartbreak baptizes you in the immersion of emotions, some of which you may have never felt before. It is your journey to take; no one can take it for you.

As I was entering into the deeper waters of all my un-grieved losses, which were touched off by the loss of my second marriage, I was told that healers are made by heart-break. There can be no healing greater than moving through the narrow passage that threatens to pull me so far beneath the surface I may not return. When I experience big personal events of grief, they open up places inside me, inviting me to tend to the hurts I haven't gotten to yet. There are always more—more oceans to cross, more salt water to suck up through my nose, more waves to thrash against, more flushing of the wounds if I choose to allow myself to flow with grief. It is my hope that we will become a culture that favors grief, rather than pushes it aside to "move on" and press into our forward plans. Grief will not drown you, and heartbreak will not break you, although it certainly feels like it will when you're dancing with hopelessness and shame.

There is tremendous fear around getting stuck with grief, and there are certainly times when depression sets in. Grieving so many events wore me down, and I felt the heavy cloak of depression around my shoulders. Much of this book began with notes in my phone when I wasn't able to get a pen to paper. I wrote "depressed" and then "de-pressed," which felt like freedom from being pressed, which evolved into "deep rest."

Healing can be a tiresome process. Prolonged or repressed grief causes a lingering malaise that can become a lifeway. When I was pregnant with my second child and worried about her birth going smoothly, my midwife reminded me that "all babies come out." I welcomed this thought, as I was initiated into what felt like the bottom of a very deep, dark well of suffering. I was in agony with the pain of loss of our marriage, dreams, hopes, and plans for the future, with the loneliness I felt as I was gestating in the womb of transformation. I reminded myself: "All babies come out." Practicing letting go helps the next practice go more smoothly.

I don't have much connection to Catholicism, or religion of any kind, but I've always admired the ritual of holy water being sprinkled on a new baby's forehead. It seems to me a welcome into a strange new world full of unimagined adventures—and, yes, heartbreak. During this year of *going through* rather than trying to go around my pain, I felt a presence protecting me, not from descending into deep grief, but from becoming fixated on the fear that I wouldn't come back from such a descent.

Healing requires faith, which can be a big ask in a world where many events do not make any sense at all. Imagine yourself accountable to your healing and the faith of your choosing, and let this be a small light on your forehead as you are transformed by loving, losing, and being rebirthed.

*I allow myself to be initiated into new form by trusting myself to be birthed by the sacred waters of my grief.*

# OF EARTH

*Our anchor, our rock,*

*our abundant provider—*

*we are born of what also reclaims us*

# PARTNERING WITH NATURE

Earth is our home: a round, full-bodied rock, 4.5 billion years old with nearly 75 percent of its surface covered in water. Earth is a mirror of our complex ecosystems; her wholeness is my wholeness and yours. I refer to Earth in the feminine because her roundness is like a pregnant womb, her waters like amniotic fluid.

According to my people of the Southeast, Earth holds creative potential, while the sun transfers the energy needed to support life. Beyond the gender binary, Earth is the feminine creative potential in all of us. From space, she looks peaceful: clothed in green, blue, and white. On our journeys through life, we seek to connect with the wholeness Earth demonstrates. Wholeness, to me, is feeling self-contained: nondependent on external people, places, or things for my contentment and completeness. It is self-supporting, but not selfish or absorbed in self-ness.

I look to this planet, our home, as a mother who nourishes and provides, who laughs through baby animals and blossoms, rages in hurricanes, and sobs in torrents of rainfall. Sometimes, finding a sense of comfort with our connection to the Earth is challenging, and we may feel disconnected from her beautiful rhythms and cycles, even if they are an intrinsic part of who we are. Often, reconnecting to Earth requires going back to the primal memory of what was true before we came into form. What we know most from before birth is the womb: the memory we cannot readily recall in language but remember through pulse and sensation, maybe even stillness and peace. Even if our carriers were stressed or stressing us, it was the time before time during which nutrients were filtered and fed to us, and our waste carried away. The warmth and heartbeat of the womb is universally appreciated and reexpressed among humans in ceremonies, rituals, and musical sounds throughout the world.

When you experience heartache, returning to the womb—symbolized in both the deep caves of the Earth and our own experience of being in utero—can help us to heal. During such times, you may crave being closer to nature and aspects of your deeper ancestry. It makes sense that we would look back to our memories of more peaceful or secure times to comfort what is difficult to metabolize now.

I often lie on the Earth like a child and ask for my complicated feelings to disintegrate. After all, dirt and plants contain enzymes and live bacteria that break down organic material into very small components. Accordingly, we need help dissolving our projections of shame and sorrow when the volume is too great to process with the limitations we may have. Our part is in yielding, in consenting and partnering with nature to midwife us through our rebirth into new forms of being; to feed our dead cells to the Earth, who can use them as fertilizer for what she is growing next.

*I continually yield to Earth's microorganisms for help with breaking down and shedding past and present trauma.*

# FINDING SAFETY

HEARTBREAK CAN RESULT FROM FEELING LIKE WE'RE not safe—whether this lack of safety is self-imposed or someone else's doing. Because safety is such a fundamental human need, when we don't have it, it is a betrayal that affects our present and future, and can also reawaken times we've felt unsafe in the past.

If you are engaging in healing yourself from a lack of safety, it is important to remember to get yourself to safety as quickly as possible—to ensure that it is a condition of your healing. Being in situations where we cannot protect ourselves is a violation of our intrinsic dignity and all that we require in order to be agents of our own healing.

We often think of physical safety when we think of being safe, because it is the most visible and obvious way to identify and legitimize a threat. Less detectable forms of harm exist, too, and we tend to tolerate longer periods of mental, emotional, psychological, and spiritual safety when there is confusion about whether or not we are truly unsafe. We may think that if we have a roof over our head, clothing, food, and a community, we are getting all that we need. While material safety is absolutely essential, we must learn to trust the deeper voice that throbs within us, that reveals the many paper cuts that have slashed away at our self-esteem or our dignity. Some forms of unsafety are not always obvious, but if we listen to the stirrings of our heart, to the signals that our body sends when we are prone to fight, flee, freeze, or appease, we may discover that an essential part of us has been endangered or harmed.

Sometimes, through repetitive acts of self-inflicted stress—overworking, drinking too much, engaging in other toxic behaviors—we find that we are the ones stripping ourselves of the safety that we need in order to heal. Regardless of who is inflicting the harm, conscious or not, we must be disciplined about the process of recovery. During healing, old wounds may reopen, and the proud flesh will need to be dressed and bandaged to ensure that we are making progress. However, our wounds will fester if we don't offer ourselves a safe space—a sanctuary that reflects the wisdom of this Earth, and the instinct in all living beings to move toward thriving and flourishing.

If you have been violated, it may be tough to feel safe again, but some form of safety, even if it's in the form of an emotional refuge you've offered yourself, is necessary in order to ground into our healing process. Draw inspiration from nests, cocoons, and underground havens into which animals burrow. Earth provides for all our mundane and spiritual needs, allowing us to rest and replenish our energies.

*I seek out and create safe spaces that allow me to flourish and create myself anew.*

# FEELING AROUND
# THE CAVE BOTTOM

HEARTACHE SOLICITS YOUR CONSENT TO FEEL THE FULL extent of your emotions. Loss—of relationships, of loved ones, of vital body parts and abilities, of dreams—leaves us with the responsibility to feel around the bottoms of our innermost caves. Like deep mines containing the detritus of past geological eras, but no sunlight, there are unknown artifacts and treasures among the rubble.

Fractured chips of your soul are often not discovered until new events lead you to seek meaning and guidance from memories and felt senses. As you evolve with more tools for deeper exploration, you'll discover parts of yourself you didn't know you had. Crawling through pitch darkness on your belly through narrow openings into subterranean realms, you are invited to find your hidden pieces via echolocation—sensing your way back through the pain to your earthly essence. You will not always feel safe, but you can create structures to support you as you explore.

The portal of grief and its accompanying suffering is an initiation into your depths. In loss, you release what you cannot keep. In retrieval, you take a new form that is born of experience. The geology of Earth is stable at its core yet responsive to fluctuation at all times. In your willingness to be present as you feel for your pieces on the cave floor, you connect with the wisdom of your core to sense what parts of yourself are calling for deeper attention and healing.

*I permit myself to stay a little bit open in heartache, trusting my fragments to be re-membered in the darkness of Earth's womb.*

# LEARNING FROM DEEP TIME

WHEN IT COMES TO HEALING DEEP HEARTACHE, WE CAN feel a sense of urgency to move the process along. I have learned through being close with Earth that evolution takes time and consistent effort. Time can be elastic, and forward movement can occur rapidly, like when you expose yourself to new teachings and perspectives or take a break from ordinary daily life to cultivate a new experience.

Healing can come quickly with a dream in which you experience a triumph of resolution or peace. Emotions can be moody and take you two steps forward, one step back. Time can move tectonically, very slowly, so it feels like very little is transforming or changing.

Geologically speaking, the transfiguration of rock depends on cooling temperatures. When rocks cool quickly, the result is glassier and less composited materials, such as obsidian. Rocks that are slower to cool tend to be more amalgamated conglomerates that maintain the diverse elements of their original components.

This interaction with time is what creates so much of what we see on the planet. *Deep time* is a term that refers to evolution, and it's similar to deep space in that it's not clear exactly what happened in the past, when we have only the tools of today with which to measure. In the process of human emotional evolution, it seems worthwhile to study time and space as you feel called, to notice what you are doing when hours feel like minutes and when days feel like lifetimes. Remember that we can be healing and changing at the same time we are moving forward. Healing isn't linear, but a living process of integration of what you have felt and what you are learning.

Nature shows us rapid change: how quickly a kitten becomes a cat, a big orange flower becomes a giant squash in the garden, rust forms on unprotected metal when wet, or mold grows on leftovers. It demonstrates how slowly shores change from rock and pebble to long stretches of sand, how long a gnarled tree can live with decades of almost no precipitation, or how long it takes your hair to grow out from an unwanted cut.

Heartache can feel geothermal, hot water churning underground. Both warming and cooling trends are impacted by our expectations of where we should be on the timeline, when we should be ready for a new relationship or try again for another child. Sometimes, even in the process of making a dramatic decision, we are still healing and changing simultaneously. Waiting for healing to take place before we can move decisively toward fulfillment can lead to inertia, stuckness. At the same time, forcing healing can create what feels like insurmountable pressure, accompanied by the unconscious need to numb ourselves from what is most uncomfortable. We must learn to navigate time with wisdom and discernment so that we can support our own healing process to the best of our ability.

 *I allow Earth's examples of deep time to help me stay in pace with my healing process.*

# LETTING GO

COLLAPSE IS A PART OF HOW WE DO LIFE. ENERGETICALLY, we fall down when we are overburdened and stand up when we experience the freedom of releasing our burdens. There is a simple joy in letting go, and it does not mean that we become severed from what matters.

Letting go can be difficult when the devastation surrounding us is at peak awareness. The prevalence of destruction is in our consciousness and heavy on our hearts. The media emphasizes stories of destruction because the media is in the business of fear-based sales. There are millions of non-newsworthy headlines that are emotionally creative or neutral. Being addicted to drama and stress, as we have been conditioned to be in order for the cogs of industry to turn, we experience endorphins and dopamine that we associate as necessary to our whole reality. We know the world is slowly burning down what hasn't proven to work. The reality is that it has always been in a state of creation or destruction, and always will be. It is the nature of existence to always be changing.

But this reality creates feelings of anxiety and angst. Events move quickly, and we move more slowly. As we learn what disastrous practices are doing to our habitat, we experience the stress of projected worries about how we will live and thrive without a healthy home. It is not unwarranted to worry, and it is not sustainable to worry full-time. Personal relationships and joys big and small must be sought to offset and relieve the stresses of existence during a rapidly moving epoch in which we are highly aware of our evolution.

Humans are circumstantial victims of being sped up beyond what our bodies and minds can tolerate. Our habitual response is to add more responsibility. When I was exhausted with the grief of loss and change, I decided to get a new dog and a new horse. These animals were welcome distractions and got me away from technology. However, the additional responsibility was not fully measured and sometimes added stress to my already overloaded mind and body. I wanted to measure the benefits of having these animals in order to justify the extra stress I was feeling. What I needed to do was eliminate some of my other commitments so I could have time and energy, critical resources, to be with my new companions and find joy in these relationships. The time I spent with them allowed me to go to sleep smelling of dog and horse, and missing out on what everyone was doing on Instagram. What I gave myself was permission to step back from the urgency of big catastrophes while I moved through the transformation period.

With more intention, I have selected three ways to be of service to my community and address the priorities with which I do have some agency. Our immediate environments and their realities show us where we are needed. We do not have to rally for every cause simply because we are aware of it. It is too much.

Identify your top areas of concern and decide how and where you can take action to help. Along with exploring the grief of your losses and the fullness of existence itself, pair these tasks with joy and peacefulness, so that you continue to generate energy for the life contained in the one body you have. Earth demonstrates how to hold the complexity of constant transformation, yet she does not force the blossoms to come before the thaw.

*I accept that collapse is part of recovery and transformation.*

# CELEBRATING DIVERSITY

EARTH IS HOSPITABLE TO COUNTLESS PLANTS, GEOLOGICAL formations, and creatures—and so many of us are so weird! If you've never seen the tardigrade, tiny waterborne bacteria that live in moss and resemble a bear, be sure to look it up.

What diverse wonders are all around us! Our perceptions can seem very small when focused on the pain in our inner landscapes. It's been estimated that the Earth hosts between five million and a trillion different species, including oceanic ones. We forget that diversity is the essence of our planet and tend to get stuck in self- or other-imposed judgments about how we should and could be. We often struggle with and judge one another's choices and idiosyncrasies, without much consideration paid to respecting our vital differences, to seeing them as an integral part of our ecosystems.

Earth is a loving mother, though her lessons are challenging to stomach at times. I turn to her not for consistency and predictability—that kind of security must be cultivated within me to face conflict. We always have the opportunity to accept that harmful behaviors are a mismatch and to adjust our proximity accordingly. Earth holds the unique expressions of the experiences that have shut our hearts down. Earth is ripe with many different life forms. She mirrors back our abilities to work and be together, enabling humanity to deliver nutrients to one another and ensure our safety, security, and joy in showing up fully, exactly as we are.

*I love and welcome differences, mine and others, with openness and imagination.*

# EMBODYING EARTH

Your nurturing connections with Earth are not transactional. They have the potential to be much more than tit-for-tat, a return on investment. The relationships we build with other humans, plants, and animals bring meaning and purpose to our lives, and are especially supportive during healing the acute pain of loss.

We can realize that as we move on Earth, *we are Earth*. We are the mother herself, nourishing ourselves with every mobilized step we take to unfold and regenerate after the death of what we cherished. We self-repair as we experience the intimacy of being held by the ground beneath us, holding a close gaze with life forms that contain medicine.

When someone close to you has died or a precious relationship has flown away, it is connection and intimacy that you miss. You knew that person as well as you were able: their flaws and weak spots, their strengths and humor. The pain of losing special people causes us to need resuscitation and reanimation. Being in nature surrounds us with reminders that we are of nature, that *we are nature*.

I have had many experiences in nature that affirm and validate my experiences. I can impregnate those experiences with meaning, and it is okay to do this. It is indigenous to immerse yourself in the imaginative creation myths of the land and our people while you find your way. Some philosophies warn against reading too much meaning into your experiences—that becoming bound by narratives that require too much magical thinking can create more suffering. You will know when you have used magical thinking too much to heal by checking whether you feel grounded in your body and if you are able to be tolerant of routine conflicts without bypassing or using spirituality as a way to dismiss what requires attention. If you must "magic" your way into feeling better, it may be time for a reality check. Earth provides this through the stability she has offered for thousands of years to the ancestors you came through.

Humans are not without bold imaginations. Our visions and imaginings have given birth to worlds of philosophy, art, and science. We make stories with our available languages to generate meaning, and to experience security of place for ourselves. Earth doesn't lie about what is happening to her. She has no need to pretend. This is encouragement that, in our story-making, we take care not to practice denial, lying, and justifying poor behavior toward ourselves and one another. Spiritual bypassing, while a temporary comfort, eventually leads to more loneliness. It is your responsibility to be whole and embodied, like Earth.

We are parts of Earth walking, moving, digesting, contemplating, and securing ourselves. Our stories will shift as we mend, mature, and actualize—shedding the faulty roles of others while confronting how we rely on mythology to support us as we traverse difficult terrain. It matters less whether the stories we tell ourselves in hurt or desperation are true. We do not need to make life-altering decisions during the healing process. What matters is to keep walking through your landscapes, building relationships with yourself and the land that feeds you, all the while creating conditions that allow for medicine to make itself.

To be embodied, we are invited to confront where we are co-reliant with Earth and where we are reliant on a false sense of security. As we mature, heal from heartbreak, and accept what isn't in our control, we can focus more on matters of spirit and soul, and whether even concepts of spirit and soul are limitations to our freedom. These deep conversations about your existence can happen directly with Earth and the natural environment surrounding you, as part of your spiritual and mundane experience.

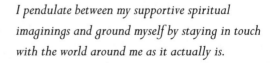

*I pendulate between my supportive spiritual imaginings and ground myself by staying in touch with the world around me as it actually is.*

# ALWAYS EVOLVING

STUDYING YOUR ANCESTORS AND THE LANDS YOUR people came from can help create inner security while you heal. Not everyone has access to ancestral records, but I'd wager that most of us have at least a little bit of information to explore. The places your people come from offer you abundant resources for healing your heartache. If your family immigrated to new worlds beyond the homelands, learning all you can about the plants, customs, and ceremonies they used to heal their communities can be so helpful.

For my Irish and Scottish ancestors, working domestic livestock, plants, and land, as well as singing songs to Earth as I work, honoring seasonal changes, and having a tall garden, keeps me close to them. I draw upon the strength they developed to persevere against tyrant monarchies before coming to the new land. My Native ancestors keep me close to very much the same things, and I hold our healing paths, food ways, creation myths, and stories in my heart to keep my imagination vivid and my body strongly bonded with the homelands. Honoring our ancestors' connections to Earth helps us to embody our medicines as we heal. As technology soars, our bodies are becoming ever more important to prioritize.

Remember that Earth is always evolving based on new conditions—and since we are Earth walking, we can choose to evolve in our approach to connecting with our deep roots. When we expose ourselves to new conditions, we are bound to evolve. The conditions of our ancestors, in a time before the intensity of migration, governmental pressures, and conflicts of civilization, are a communal playground for us to connect to ourselves and them. It may require some excavation, but it is time well spent. Earth and her resulting cultures are a library of knowledge, wisdom, and practices available to each of us.

The colonial imagination is limited and bound by historical motivations of self-preservation, intense survival, and deep fear. In what ways does surviving colonial capitalism limit you? What are your goals and priorities today, and what would they be if you were not so focused on paying the bills and making a retirement plan? If you remember that you are Earth walking, what new rules will you create and recover from your wise ancestors?

*I excavate the stories of my people to bring security to my healing and my existence.*

# SAVING US FROM US

SAVING THE EARTH HAS BEEN A BATTLE CRY AMONG environmentalists and climate activists. I recognize the sentiment, but I don't see how this can be true. Earth has been here for billions of years and will be here long after we're gone. Earth is not responsible for failing to keep our home in good working order; we humans are.

Organized religion is full of concepts like "salvation" and "redemption," but what do they really mean as it pertains to saving our burning house? Greed, extraction, exploitation, industrialization—these motivators have shoved us into a tight spot in which we have become complicit. While not all extreme weather events have been caused by humans, there is enough compelling evidence to confirm that most of our climate-related events have been. This is understandably causing a lot of worry.

When I was growing up, adults around me were very concerned with getting to heaven. The afterlife was of utmost importance, and everyone was attempting to earn their way into it. Salvation occurred by means of a mediator who had jurisdiction over souls and helped them "'get right with God," so they could be ensured a seat at the royal table in the sky. This idea of salvation by an external mystical force feels misguided to me; we seem to require saving from ourselves.

While we distract ourselves with finger-pointing and scapegoating, we have allowed greed, denial, and exploitation to destroy what we need to keep living. This has resulted in a gloomy forecast for the coming generations. We are in a toxic shame spiral caused by not keeping industry in check, because our own desire for goods, security, luxury, and compulsions are taking precedence. Climate instability has complex roots in half a dozen generations, and tracking and repairing is harder to comprehend than simply blaming others for what we are still participating in. This is complex multigenerational trauma we're talking about.

What we have forgotten how to do in all of these decades is work together in our areas of strength and demonstrate the courage to change. It is heartbreaking to accept our ongoing role in systems of destruction. The same energy that got us into a climate mess must be wielded to get us out of it. How might that work? First, we must accept that it will take several generations to slow the impact of extreme climate events. We can groom our internal landscapes for decades of patience and pace, two qualities technology has challenged us to discard in exchange for stressful urgency. However, we can take a lesson from our powerful mother, who doesn't require a knight in shining armor, but rather, our own awakening to our interconnectedness, which begins within.

> *I give up external saviorism and rescue my inner landscape from conditional suffering.*

# INTEGRATING THE MYSTERY

THE COMPLEX BEAUTY FOUND IN NATURE SOOTHES SCAR tissue and brokenheartedness. There is hidden wisdom in the spiral center of each floral expression, packed golden onto the legs of honeybees, dripping from cloud formations, collecting green-scalloped and fur-like on granite boulders, in the bright pelleted eyes of a jet-black raven who communicates with more than a hundred vocalizations.

Earth is constantly holding and healing our hearts through her allure and pulsing reverberations. By divine inspiration through creation and evolution, the heartbeat of Mother Earth is embodied in you, and it drums within you. She knows there is no metric for spiritual success. Nature implores you to be at peace with this lack of measurable results by offering its ever-changing seasons and tides—reminders that while we can track some aspects, nature in its complexity remains mysterious.

The mystery is perfectly imperfect, coiled within magnificent mundanity: Every new life birthed through the generations, every river that deposits into the ocean, every tree that drops its leaves in the winter and resurrects in the spring, all contingent on how long freezes last and how hard the wind blows. There is predictability to this rhythm, like the timed thump of a persistent drum, which can be heard and felt when we place our ears against the ground or a beloved's chest. However, the variations are always new.

Our hearts break a little each time the garden bounty fades, and yet there are small seeds, the remainders of the ordinary champions that bring the promise of next year's crops. Your ancestors moved seasonally—they had no other option but to arrange their existences around plants, sunshine, water, mountains, and wildlife. Even with such incalculable complexity, there is simplicity. The fear, heartbreak, and chaos that humanity experiences amid natural and forced changes can be met with presence—acceptance that life, and its trillions of forms, is in perpetual motion.

The ecological demise fatigue that abounds these days can add to your weariness. Remember to be heartened that Earth has been through 4.5 billion years of change. Does she grieve the loss of jungles where there are now painted desert hills? Does she lament the dry creek beds where prehistoric mammals came to drink? In a unique way all her own, she might. While we see evidence of Earth adapting to changes beyond her control, we also comprehend her acceptance.

Earth is gracious in matters of recovery and transformation. To be earthed is to become like rock: not immovable or unchangeable, but anchored by a power greater than herself. Her gravity comes from a community of intricately placed fellow celestial bodies throughout the infinite cosmos. We can lean into this supportive network to recognize that we, too, are cosmic beings—constantly evolving and learning to integrate even more of the mystery.

*I employ my infinite, galactic imagination to help me lean into grief while adapting to change.*

# KNOWING WE ARE HELD

EARTH IS GOOD COMPANY TO KEEP, ESPECIALLY WHEN we're aching. Animals provide companionship and heart coherence, a state that occurs when the heart and brain are deeply connected and harmonious. When we feel the pain of separation, it is like being caught in a web of illusion. This state compounds the agony of grief.

Meditating on feelings of connectedness while sitting in a park or under a tree has helped me feel held by Earth and part of something greater than myself. In loss, we isolate our emotions, holding them close to our chest while experiencing the drama of difference. We are fragmented by our experiences, fractured from connection to something or someone that mattered very much to us.

In this culture, we have come to know drama as extreme states—highs and lows characterized by out-of-control emotions. It is an act of courage to be with ourselves through these extreme feelings. Being with Earth helps us to be on Earth. Earth vibrates at an average frequency of 7.83 Hertz. This is sometimes called the Schumann resonance, after physicist Winfried Otto Schumann, who predicted this in mathematical terms in 1952. Attuning to this electromagnetic pulse can help regulate our body's and brain's systems by putting us into a theta brain-wave state as we sync with Earth's heartbeat.

It may be similar to how we felt in the womb while our carriers were in a resting state. The theta brain-wave state is conducive to lucid visioning or dreams, and we can direct it by priming ourselves with thoughts that we belong on Earth, because we *are* on Earth. It may sound simple to affirm reality, but in times of uncertainty when emotions are running high, the easiest reassurances can feel supportive. Companion animals or equine therapy can help us by calming our energies and offering loving gazes and touch when we struggle with feelings of separateness. Earth self-regulates and is a model for how we can self-regulate, too. Earth cradles us while we tend ourselves.

*I connect to my environment and creatures of*
*Earth to remind myself that I am not alone.*

# DIGGING A GRAVE

DEATH IS A PART OF LIFE THAT IS STILL VERY DIFFICULT to be at peace with. The loss of a beloved presence and body in our lives is felt as a missing, a gap in our beingness, a hole in our hearts.

Metabolizing the actual loss of a loved one can take a long time. We anticipate and sometimes continue to hear their footsteps and voices in our homes after they are gone. When someone who has not physically died has gone away, it can still feel like a death. Burial is a way to ritualize and lay to rest what can no longer be in physical form.

The day before my fiftieth birthday, two months after my marriage ended, a large owl flew into a tree in my backyard while hunting, and I didn't see where it landed. Hours later, I saw it sitting upright in a stone circle my former partner had assembled for me, eyes blinking from being stunned and trying to protect itself from my worried presence. I phoned the local wild animal rehab center, who asked me to place it in a cardboard box with a towel; they would try to dispatch someone in the morning. I do not place wild animals in cardboard boxes, but I do phone friends and family to ask what they would do. All agreed that I should pray for myself and leave it alone.

I prayed all afternoon, its suffering mirroring mine. I felt that it was an omen about what was dying that I could not, and should not, try to resuscitate. As I wept at a distance, the owl shifted and turned its body. I could see that there was a large gray bull snake dead in its talons. My mind hurried to make meaning out of this symbol of a double death in my sacred circle—and at that, of two powerful animals that I had been studying for many years. I prayed all night, made offerings of tobacco near the circle, and wept and wept and wept. I wanted so much for the owl to live.

Through the night, I heard an owl calling out a five-hoot sound-off. Typically, there is a responding screech from the mate in the pair. Tonight, there was no answer. I wept some more. I finally put myself to bed, still in prayer, asking for what could not be granted: for this owl to find courage in its partner's call—and by some miracle, some act of Creator, find a surge of energy and be reunited.

The next morning, I went out, and even as I was walking, I was praying, hoping I wouldn't see its figure. The owl had walked to the center of the circle and fallen over dead in the night. I made more offerings and buried it where it had fallen, and I did the same with the snake. When I called a close friend to tell her how it had turned out and how deeply undone I was that I didn't have the magical powers of resurrection I wish I'd had, she said, "It's dead, baby." As I dug, I wept. I accepted all I could in the moment, which was not much, but it was the beginning of integrating immense love with immense loss. I was soaked in the rain with the rich smell of cinnamon-colored Earth filling my senses, and as the shovel head sunk into the dirt over and over, I prayed for myself to let go of what I could not keep alive.

We do not typically bury in a way that allows Earth to reclaim and repurpose our bodies. Part of our collective denial is in preserving the bodies of our dead so that we do not have to face their decomposition. Somehow, we have agreed, in policy and practice, to protect and retain physicality. I believe this hinders grieving what is gone. Prolonging the inevitable is a coping mechanism that has great cost to the planet.

When we have lost love, a dream, a treasured position or role, our health, or a relationship, we also prolong the release. We mourn and mourn in a very long wake of wishing that things could be the way they were before. We do not allow ourselves to move forward, opting instead to remain in bondage to the past, leaving some of our vital life force back there with it, as if it is carrying on in a merry way in a different dimension while we are stuck in this miserable one. Avoiding or prolonging the burial of pain that is not connected to the loss of a loved one's life or body is emotionally logical, because there may not be anything physical that you are willing to let go. Photos, cards, jewelry, talismans, even sports equipment, are clutched like a rosary as we try to pray a different reality to life. The energy it takes to grasp is well spent in uncurling each frozen finger and giving the past to the one who is biologically most competent to transmute it.

*I will dig a grave for what is gone with great love, so that Earth can do the holding.*

# WITH AIR

*Sacred breath of life*
*animating force of all cells*
*taken in until it is taken from us*

# RESPONDING TO THE WINDS OF CHANGE

AIR IS A VERSATILE ELEMENTAL TEACHER, BECAUSE while it is made up of simple atmospheric particles, it's always changing. The wind is seen as free and unencumbered by containment; it cannot be harnessed or forced, and we cannot see it, much like our thoughts and how we experience ideas, and even spirits.

We refer to the wind as a change bringer. We intend to "see which way the wind blows" while we gather more information before making a decision. The wind is transient, informed by offshore storms. The wind is invisible, seemingly without form, yet sweeps down the sides of mountains and across prairies, bends trees over, and carries rain and fire forth.

When I think of wind as an influence while tending heartbreak, I think of the "winds of change" and how when I have stood facing the wind, of which there is much in the high desert region where I live, it freshens me, almost as if it's offering to blow off what I've let become stuck to me. Sometimes, wind threatens to carry me off to Oz like Dorothy and Toto. Either way, wind is the signature of shifts and pivots, of unforeseen fates ahead. It is a game of watch and wait and see what happens. To be prepared while battening down the hatches.

It is in this state, at this transient and unpredictable crossroads, close to the elements that come and go, that I feel some excitement about new things, even while I am still processing the past. It is also a time of attuning to my intuition about what I can begin to release, what I can become more free about.

Ideas about how to transition into the next phases of life, hobbies, and plans tickle like a breeze on your cheek as you feel gently into your emotions about the person, dream, or love you lost, while also embracing that life is moving on ahead and you are willing to go with it. The wind invites us not to dwell so much in the past where we cannot change others or situations, but to pay attention to the messages it carries, like pollen and seeds, for what is to come.

*I can grieve the past and also listen to what is whispering me forward.*

# PLAYING THE FOOL

HEARTACHE LASTS FOR THE MOONS IT LASTS, AND EVEN after that, a gust can come through and knock you down. Grief is a wheel and also a compass. The catalyst for heartbreak is the rupture, a journey that is often unwanted.

Breath, wind, thunder, the infinite sky—all of the wildness and freedom that air symbolizes brings us back to beginning again with a new mind. I think of the Fool in the tarot, pictured with his knapsack tied to a stick and slung over his shoulder, eyes up, little dog nipping at his heels, ready for a new adventure, new perspectives, new ways of thinking. This archetype helps me when I think of the resentment of my unexpected physical and emotional whiplash—the feeling of being spun around in the wind, hanging like a plastic sack caught in a tree.

The lessons have been learned as much as they can for this time. Last year's cares have all but blown away, and our systems feel ready to greet the dawn again. No one likes to think of themselves as a fool, but love that leaves can make us feel vulnerable, self-doubting. This resistance is also why proud flesh stays so rigid. It stands in a gale-force wind on the hill it's willing to die on, about how the other person didn't care, didn't stay, didn't do better—triggering all of our childhood hurts and tossing us away.

But what are the benefits of being a fool? Is it acceptable to be a fool for love of this process, of staying with yourself, not leaving, not abandoning yourself, not knowing what the outcome will be but moving forward anyway? You can take the next right step just for today, minding your footing a little more this time, protecting but not overprotecting. You can be open enough and young-spirited enough to let the breeze gently kiss your face and hold you in the ways you want to be held—to have your experiences validated. It is love that breaks our hearts, and it is always love that heals us.

*I allow fresh air to blow through my spirit as I love myself into aliveness.*

# NOTICING OUR BREATH

YOUR BREATH IS A HUG YOU GIVE YOURSELF ABOUT twenty thousand times per day. Breath awareness teaches us to notice our breathing and how our thoughts influence our breath. Stressful moments cause our bodies to shorten and quicken the breath, which impacts our hearts, blood pressure, and brains. When we react to stressful stimuli, we don't hug ourselves with full intimacy. Our breath becomes like a brief one-armed pat, rather than a full embrace.

Our organs need the fullness of our breath to function optimally. I've found that there is a catch right at my heart center when I'm dysregulated or sliding into a state of non-awareness. We don't have to be conscious all the time; after all, air is going to deliver breath to us, whether we're paying attention or not. In times of stress, paying attention can help you maintain connection between your brain and your body so that your responses will come from a more regulated place. Opening up the tight places with the breath, letting the facial muscles relax and the shoulders drop, is simply a way of tending your body with an aware mind rather than the defensiveness of the brain.

The brain has many useful parts, and the ones that jump into action when you're stressed help when you're in legitimate danger. Emotional distress happens far more often than life-threatening danger occurs, and it is not sustainable for your health to strain with physical reactions each time you have an emotional alarm go off, however small. Oxygen circulating gently through your body's systems will help you register danger in a more practical manner. Tending breath allows you to pause before reacting, take the time you need, and acknowledge that your beautiful, complex brain is readying for a situation that isn't actually happening. Experiencing heartache is a time when more alarm bells of distress are going off than usual. Breath is balancing. Imagine that it requires your conscious mind to ease your heart and support circulation, so your heart can nurture the parts of your brain that feel understandably afraid.

*I hug myself more intentionally with my breath when I need it most.*

# SOFTENING THROUGH
# THE CONSTRICTION

Tensile and strong, we are able to do what the Western world loves to praise; that is, we find ourselves "powering through" difficult times. Running on autopilot or superhero strength is always expected of "lady bosses" and people of the Fortune 500, with no regard for what their productivity costs them in health, emotional and spiritual well-being, and intimacy with their loved ones.

Yes, we humans can power through—and it is a most helpful skill when it is used in the short term to get through the immediate tasks at hand. Over long periods, hyper-strengthening has a tightening effect—cutting off the flow of oxygen to whatever within us is still seeking healing.

The tissue is pale at the site where the wound is held, and my body has experienced problems in places like these. Where there is constriction, there is no air or blood flow. Our parts are cut off from the whole, separated and overprotected, if not strangulated.

Breathe deep and long into these areas, bringing conscious awareness into the constricted focal points, warming them with your breath and even physical touch. Let your breath be deep and prolonged over tight areas; this is akin to the act of stretching muscles that have been engaged in heavy lifting, giving them space and the opportunity for repair. Growth happens on the emotional and spiritual level when you work an area and give equal time to relaxing it with the spaciousness of your care and attention.

*I allow oxygen to infuse my cells with life force, breathing into the constricted places in my body that have grown tight with fear.*

# BREATHING OUR WHOLENESS

THE ACHE AND STRESS OF LOSS, ABANDONMENT, AND terror steals the breath. The wind is knocked out of us as a blow to the chest cavity. Our rib baskets house and protect the diaphragm, which carries oxygen into the depths of our pelvic bowl, where the organs of reproduction and creativity reside.

Injuries to the pelvic bowl—through giving birth, sexual mishandling and assault, self-neglect, and hyper-movement—begin cutting off our breath from the bottom up. Over time, the breath becomes shallow, reaching the solar plexus or stomach area before contracting back into an exhalation.

In the West, we do not know how to breathe properly. Breath carries energy far beyond the shallow inhalations we rely upon to resource our bodies with healing oxygen and a sustainable pace. Sipping breath in short samples is what we do in survival, panting in scarcity, while diaphragmatic breath, the holy whole breath of our ancestors, is an experience in which our entire rib basket fills with abundant life force that is sent to our vital organs and creative zones.

With practice, we can feel our breath carrying oxygen to our extremities. In this way, air reclaims us from our gasping and holding. We must bring our hearts to how we breathe. Try it now: Summon air in through your nose, filling the lower lungs, bringing it all the way up the channel, noticing any catches, and back out with your exhale like a slow bellows from the bottom of the lungs up. Do this when you feel stressed, dissociated, or like you are not fully inhabiting yourself.

*I am reclaimed by the depth of my breath,*
*which infuses the whole of me and reassures my*
*dismembered parts, easing them back together.*

# SPRING CLEANING
# FOR THE BODY AND SPIRIT

FRESH AIR IN YOUR SPACES IS LIKE SPRING FINALLY arriving after a long winter. Opening the windows to clear out stagnancy of eyes, body, and spirit is a favorite ritual here in the north that I took for granted when I lived in a milder climate. Greeting each new dawn is a welcome re-union, and the morning air does the spirit good.

I wonder if you've ever thought of letting go of all of your belongings, except for just what you need to create a new beginning. I used to know exactly what little cast-iron skillet I would choose, and how I couldn't live without my stainless-steel tea strainer (I can make sun tea out of many random plants) in my new fantasy life all alone in the wild. I kept a list of which two books I would bring along and whether I should remove the hardback covers to lighten my load—and could I get everything into a backpack?

Alas, apart from weekend camping, I have yet to de-clutter my life to the point where I could carry all my necessities on my back. It's funny how I still carry emotions around with me in a Santa-sized sack, because I do not yet know how to release some of them. Family photos used to be in a big album or two on the coffee table, with a stash of really old ones in a cardboard box in the attic. We had to choose which ones we were going to keep—and of those, which ones to display and which to store. My phone currently has 51,982 photos and videos on it. I even keep the blurry ones! It has been difficult to prioritize what to let go of. I am guilty of emotional hoarding.

Spring-cleaning our emotions is a task that requires noticing them, taking an inventory of sorts, and releasing them. We will always have memories in our hearts from people, dreams, and past loves, but we do not need to hoard every emotion related to them. Opening the windows of my heart and letting the wind carry out spent emotions is both verbal and physical for me. Speaking what I am complete with doesn't magically remove the feeling from me, but in a way, it diffuses its power over me. It allows my attachment to the feeling to breathe. It enables me to connect my mind to my heart—and when the emotion is less strong, my mind and heart can decide together whether it is useful to keep it or sweep it. Either way, you can dust off feelings you had earlier in the experience of heartbreak and check in with yourself about how you feel now. To speak your intention about what you are letting go of is to get it prepared to be on its way out.

*I can declutter my emotions and clear out what I'm unconsciously hanging on to as I heal.*

# TENDING OUR MOODS

IN THIS HEALING PROCESS, I FIND A LOT OF REPETITIVE visitors: longing, sadness, desperation, anger, frustration, fear. Some people find it helpful to create digital mood and vision boards from magazine scraps or Pinterest collections to help focus their minds on positive outcomes and away from the compulsive loops. While we don't have ultimate control over outcomes, we can absolutely tend our moods. We can train our brains to spend more time in playgrounds and with people who share our visions for what we're growing and who we're growing into.

Planning a garden, gathering seeds, preparing ground— all of these bountiful possibilities start in the mind. If we can see it, we can start to live into it. Currently, I feel like a rusty old garden gate too tired to hang straight. Still, beyond this dismal feeling, I can get a little bit excited about something lush that's just for me. I have begun to notice that I can allow doors to open without beating them down. This way, I can assess a situation to see if it fits where I am going with my life. The waiting stage can be restless, so I occupy myself with mental jobs and projects in the meantime.

We cannot control the timing of events, but we can create conditions that invite them in. Putting ourselves in spaces where our visions have more space to grow is a way to ground our visions into reality. Native traditions of retreating, fasting, sitting on a mountain or in an altar for several days, and allowing for a vision can help us be with ourselves through uncomfortable stillness to prepare the body and mind for purposes that are only beginning to become known. When we gather in community, we can pool our resources for shared visions and create spaces and programs that we couldn't do alone.

Creating the world we want to live in begins with closing doors that have nothing for us behind them and being ready for others to open. If we know what we need, or what we desire more of, we will recognize it when we come upon it. We can also be open to opportunities that bear an energetic kinship to what we would like to experience during various stages of life.

In the realm of air, of the mind, what experiences can you imagine enjoying? Experiences that will help you continue growing, healing, changing, and coping with whatever happens that is not to your liking? Ideas are like breezes: They come and go. Old ideas that haven't worked out can be on their way. Sharing ideas with others and processing verbally helps to foster new beginnings as you are healing.

Get curious about where you stand, right now. What doors are you holding open that have distressing thoughts on the other side? What patterns do you continue to entertain? If you could choose to pass through a different door instead of the same old ones time after time, what do you envision you will find? What feelings and sensations are you seeking more of?

*I start slowly with new ideas and interests until the time comes for me to start building.*

# PAUSING TO CLEAR THE AIR

AIR IS AN ELEMENT OF HEALING THAT OFFERS CLARITY. We "clear the air" with caring communication, amends, reflections, validations of our and others' experiences, and bringing truth to strenuous situations.

Truth is subjective, influenced by our feelings. Heartache can inform our opinions and hurt can influence the language we use, shaping how we speak. I have many times lashed out in hurt and resentment before I have become thoughtful about the impact of my words. There are times to throw caution to the wind and say your piece. As we heal, transform, mature, and grow, it becomes easier to pause to take a breath. In this way, we can slow down the pace of painful emotions that turn into words.

Clearing the air is an artform that requires skills most of us did not receive during our formative periods. In my family, words were flung and hurts swept under the rug. I yearned for resolution, and as a result, I grew into an adult who overexplains in an attempt to be understood. This is a trauma response, and the other side of the coin to going silent. During this year of heartache and healing, I have at times said more than I wanted to. Then I had to go back and clean up the messes I'd created when I didn't pause for clarity.

It was a messy process to double back, and I offer grace to myself for having childhood wounds of not being heard or understood. It is okay to be cloudy and emotional while in struggle. Grief calls for keeping it real, and yet, at some point, we want to do better. I wanted to stop doubling back. As a verbal processor, I often cannot land on the truth until I've spoken plentifully and can tease out what I'm really trying to get at. This is tough, because part of me is urging me to make my point. The pressure can feel intense, like a can of soda that's been shaken and has trapped bubbles trying to burst out.

In these times, I sit and settle, care for myself, write my feelings and thoughts down to become more empty, and circle the points that feel true and important. I like to use the approach with myself where I discern what's true and leave the narratives and unnecessary context behind. (Perhaps this is why writing is my vocation and my editor stays very busy!) Clarity is not the most important quality, but it helps when it comes to communication with ourselves and with others when it's time to share.

If the mind has crossed wires and is sending mixed messages from states of confusion or urgency, you can slow down and go through the untangling process. Doing the labor of clearing the air of our thoughts helps clear the air within, prevents outbursts, and simplifies communication.

*I seek to understand how I communicate and where I would like to be more honest and clear.*

# DAYDREAMING OUR WAY TO CLARITY

Exploring our mental and intellectual realms is an adventure in learning how our minds work. Dreams, daydreams, ruminations, and what comes up in meditation are all fertile playgrounds for understanding ourselves and the context we're growing in. They bring hidden emotions into consciousness and produce clues about where we have basic needs.

Some material in dreams is more useful than others and can act as a guide for what we're struggling with. We can bring attention to what our mind lands on when it's allowed to wander. If you were a daydreamer in school, there may have been consequences for what was perceived as pointless or vacant thoughts when your focus was expected. Today, you can make time for dreams and random thoughts whenever possible, and let them show you what's asking for attention, or in what area you're loitering that wants inquiry. Meandering through your thoughts while experiencing feelings of heartache help you connect with what is floating to the surface from deeper places within you.

When I'm unfocused, and my attention blurry and diffused, the same gripes tend to come up that I haven't come to peace with. I can shoo these thoughts away, but they end up sneaking back up on me. At some point, I have to write about them, process them with a friend, and try not to assign too much meaning to them while exercising curiosity. When my attention hovers over betrayals, this is a sign for me to take a step back, engage my intuition and my heart, and see if there are untreated, unhealed parts trying to be heard.

When I focus my mental attention a little deeper, some parts of me want to distract me with cravings, which are flags that mark where our needs were not met, or where we experienced abandonment or rejection; they also show us where we are seeking to feel desired and accepted, and to find a sense of belonging and connection.

Fulfilling unexamined cravings sometimes comes at a cost, especially when we are avoiding or misunderstanding the prompts. Getting caught in even a light tornado of repetitive thoughts and cravings can create frustration—other hurt parts may want to shut the inquiry process down entirely out of fear. Our mental capacities are accustomed to carrying most of the load; after all, the demand on thinking our way through a challenge is high in the information age, where fixes and solutions are in front of us with every internet search.

Inner inquiry that engages the intuitive senses can be as simple as asking yourself if a challenge finds you wanting to step forward or step back. Daydreaming around this, wandering the terrain of your mind, can show you what feels dangerous (although you can determine if it really is), what you want more of and why, and what doesn't feel quite right. When our minds work collaboratively with our hearts, we can detach from looping thoughts driven by feelings, and use discernment rather than craving to make choices we can live with.

Dreams and daydreams point the way to deeper realms of the mind. It's okay if there are parts of the mind that don't feel as stable or secure; other parts can offer reasonable assurances, and the heart can offer constructive comfort.

*I allow my mind to drift and wander undirected to explore wherever it lands.*

# SEEING THE BIRD'S-EYE VIEW

Do you ever find yourself contemplating an idea or decision, or thinking about something when a bird flies by? I have an overactive mind, so this happens very often for me. Depending on the kind of bird, I will sometimes take it as a certain type of sign.

Corvids remind me to use creative, thoughtful language to communicate. Kestrels remind me to study something more deeply before taking action. Vultures remind me to save my finite energy and coast. Bald eagles, always fishing in ponds and rivers here, remind me to marry my mind to my emotions so I can be in integrity. Birds are validating this way. They fly in just when my overactive mind is getting lost in wormholes. Their visits are like a meditation bell that wakes me from my reverie and brings me back to reality.

With the amount of time most birds spend in the air, I think about what they see from up there that I'm missing from down here, engulfed in the drama of my experience. A "bird's-eye view" is emotionally detached just enough to see the big picture with a little more discernment than when facing a situation directly. Total emotional detachment or dissociation for the purpose of avoidance isn't what birds teach. They inspire me to connect my mind (air) with my heart (fire) with my emotions (water) with my body (earth) and see what changes I can observe in myself and the world around me.

It's easy to get caught up in certain ideas that are repeated day after day, and they become beliefs without our consent. I read a meme today: "Love is not a battlefield," and if you grew up in the eighties and you had only one FM rock station that played Pat Benatar every hour, that stuff is hardwired. Music perpetuates many heartbreaking realities, but seldom do songs tell us in three to four minutes how to work with, and move beyond, those emotions. When I'm in a ditch with a heartbreak (or there's a tear in my beer), I need an elevated perspective. I look to the sky, my upper mental faculties, and its messengers to help me comprehend with my heart that there is life beyond the lowlands of heartache. The return of birds in the spring presents support for new beginnings, new perspectives, new outlooks, and big-picture considerations.

*I look to the skies and frequent fliers for inspiration and breakthroughs.*

# WEATHERING LIFE'S STORMS
# WITH WONDER

WE HUMANS ARE A LITTLE BIT HERO-OBSESSED. WHEN I was growing up, my brother and I watched *Super Friends* every day after school. DC Comics and the Hall of Justice prompted my hopes when the world around me left me feeling powerless. I especially loved Firestorm, a lesser-known superhero with superhuman durability; density control allowed him to transmute his molecular structure and pass through any solid object. My favorite superpower was Firestorm's ability to fly without a cape. Batman and Superman needed special equipment to fly, but Firestorm needed only his imagination to become airborne and be on the moon within seconds. I carried a desire to harness the wind and ride the lightning, because I believed I might be able to if I could just envision it.

The juxtaposition of hero culture and what I think of as the great cosmic joke is about how much and how little power we have. Healing heartache requires super strength and durability to accept what you don't have control over and your inability to change the past. It also requires your belief that you have the fortitude and power to direct your future.

People are not gods and are not designed to be conquerors or manipulators of the elements. We cannot own the skies or lay claim to them. My child mind didn't know that I could be in awe of heroics and not need to obtain that kind of power. I could simply be inspired. Sometimes, borrowing strength from the sky and utilizing the power of our imaginations are life-saving adaptations, especially for children. Thunder and lightning live in us as booming and electrifying creative forces. By engaging their energies, we learn to weather the storms of life in a spiritual manner familiar to how our ancient ancestors navigated the world.

We need not conquer or colonize the Sky Nation as we have done with Earth, but carry with us an attitude of admiration and wonderment. Einstein described his relationship with God as a practice of being in awe of the universe. Connecting to a power greater than yourself that you lean into, that you feel humble in the presence of, is part of receiving unseen support for heartache.

Today, we are defining new ways of practicing spirituality that are not dictated by oppressive, dissociative, manipulative forces that prey on our fear, trauma, and vulnerability. A commitment to awe can help you shed nonreciprocal attachments to people, places, and things that reinforce pain (or inordinate amounts of temporary, pleasure-inducing endorphins), and reclaim connection to yourself by acknowledging the sacred and divine within you. By releasing what you are clinging to, experiences you need not own or covet, you build a bridge into a vast universe that plugs you into what is ultimate, omniscient, immanent.

I laugh at myself a lot remembering that I am but a tiny speck in the universe, bumping up against other tiny specks and becoming agitated by them. While I would much rather bond than bump up against, sometimes the nature of matter is to attract or repel. Transforming heartache is superheroic in its way, and it is also perfectly mundane to accept what we can and cannot remain bonded to. With the power we do have, we can marry our hearts and minds in self-supporting kinship with All That Is. We can detach from details and expand our vision into the stars.

*I build a bridge between the matters of my heart and the universe of my awe-inspired mind.*

# RECEIVING INFINITY

WE CANNOT BE STUDENTS OF THE ELEMENTS WITHOUT acknowledging the vast, infinite nature of the sky. Residence of heavenly bodies, planets, sun, stars, and all galactic and cosmic matter, the sky is referenced in literature, art, and in our consciousness as limitless. We associate the sky with eternal life, as promised by religions and metaphysics. It has captivated the attention and engaged the imaginations of seeking minds for thousands of years.

When you look up to the unobstructed sky, you take in the softness of clouds, the peace of its blue like a blanket on your soul. The sky is a mostly quiet space uncluttered by humans and our many still and movable structures. A daily sense of peace can come when waking to welcome the blushing dawn or bask in a coral sinking sun that takes the light we rely on with it. The sky is the vault of heaven, the realm of superior beings and mythical gods containing the upward projections of our own endless spirits. Ultimately, we yearn to feel that wide open and eternal. Simultaneously, promises of a peaceful afterlife have been a powerful tool of manipulation. While the sky promises all the infinite possibilities of a clear, blank slate, the human mind is bound by ideas that we are better in our spirits than in our bodies.

As an inspiring force of nature, and a prevalent feature in our systems of salvation that places peace in the afterlife, the sky offers respite from being tied to the rigors of life on the ground. But mass dissociation is not what we're going for. We do not want to lean so far into one medicinal ingredient—externalizing the spirit and sending it up to a detached and free-floating realm—that it overpowers our integrative healing process. Embodying cosmology is recognizing the universe within you while remaining part of it. The more we clutter our spiritual minds with oppressive rules and conditions, the more we will want to escape. Heaven is right here on Earth, in these flawed and fragile bodies.

Is it our cosmic nature to unwind internal freedom while bravely tussling with our human traumas and dramas? If freedom is defined as an absence of subjugation, then might we bring attention to where we are imprisoning ourselves and others with restrictive ideologies such as barriers, binaries, and biases? How can we integrate our experiences by bringing our surrendered will into the realm of the liberated imagination? And how can we seed new possibilities that will someday flourish and provide the healing that will support us in all our relations?

*I experience my infinite nature as eternal love expressed through a complex universe.*

# TO TAKE WITH YOU ON YOUR JOURNEY

WHAT FINALLY HAPPENED FOR ME AT THE END OF THE writing of this book, *because* of writing it all down, is that I finally gave up, or rather, I gave in. I surrendered my will, my invulnerability, and my resistance so that I could experience liberation by being with myself through the most difficult of quaking ruptures. I paid for my freedom by relinquishing my intense desire to change what I had no power, no right, and no jurisdiction over. I'd wanted the pain to stop, but I could not stop it and also stay alive. I wanted the people involved to speak and act honorably—I could not bargain, force, guilt, shame, or people-please this into existence. I had to give up the fight for security that I was having with myself—that I thought I was having with someone else. In doing so, I was able to release myself from the hook I'd hung myself on.

I traded my steely drive to change outcomes for the peace of cruising one day at a time. I swapped my bitterness for sweeter love and acceptance of myself. I have fewer answers than I did the day my marriage died face-down in the gravel driveway and fractured my family life. Again. I ended up with less knowledge, but a little more serenity. Less certainty, but a little more trust. Fewer plans for the future, but more presence. Surely, I am the result of all who have gone before me on this path of staying openhearted, of breaking down in order to break open, to become unbroken after shattering. We do not have to disconnect from life to process the past. We can make repairs and re-bond with ourselves, and not dance in the doorways with our vulnerability. We can get all in, even as people with beautiful parts come and go according to their capacity, willingness, ability to be honest, and skills. One of the most critical nutrients of an emotionally satisfying life is closeness. We must cultivate it within ourselves to move forward with confidence. But we never need to have it all figured out.

Enduring heartache that you believe might kill you is a journey every soul takes in some form, it is a rite of passage, and it matures us to come through our most harrowing ordeals. These times of collapse, lingering in liminal spaces, open us to new possibilities. It's an advanced-level skill to hold love and hurt together, to walk through bad weather with both clutched to your heart, to love what was and to also move forward.

Coming in hot with big scars and big triggers around untreated, unhealed pain is an invitation to take yourself around the wheel and through the elements to engage the surges, sensations, and terrors—not to hurry to the other side, but to get into your heart and experience how it makes medicine with your attention to self-compassion, coherence, and attunement.

May you keep your hearts open through hardship. May you stay with the tensile scars that become silkier with time, the fiery rage that becomes drifting tendrils of smoke, the engulfing salt water that eventually evaporates, the holes in the earth into which your energy and will to live plummet, only to steam upward into the sky when the season changes. May you create, burn up, and feel warmed by fire. May you stop fighting the pounding waves and allow yourself to coast, float, and surf, allowing your salty agitations to have a voice. May you lie on the earth, ground your experience, let gravity hold you down, hit your knees, find at long last the power in your body to be with the anxiety and depression that accompany the ache. May you allow your breath to do its job, let the wind sling your hair into your eyes, and confront the gale forces that are sure to come before the softness of the breeze.

You may no longer consider yourself a healer once you feel mostly healed, and that is as it should be after a humbling reckoning. You may find your long-held identities to be confining. Whatever changes occur, you will always have the agency, and the elements within and without, to heal yourself again and again, which will contribute to healing the conditions with which humanity struggles.

Be willing to look in every corner and under all the rugs and closets to find the lost parts of you that were stashed and swept into the cracks and crannies. They are waiting for the thick medicinal salve of your patient, loving attention. Stay with your heart in all weather. Stay warm.

*Love,*
Pixie

# ACKNOWLEDGMENTS

This book would not have been possible without the loving care, support, and patience of: Julie, Jennette, Anahata, Shannon, Justin, Chris E., Boise, Anne, Kina, Shanan, Tanya, Allison, Bella, Maribel, Raquel, Lorenzo, Linda, Tanya, Faith, Makalapua, Cinnamon, Holli, Donnie, Spring, Miles, Ivy, Joe, JP, Nirmala, V., Kristen, and Rebekah; the works of Mirabai Starr, Christena Cleveland, Rowen White, Martín Prechtel, Matthew Fox, and Richard Rohr; and the grace of Row House Publishing.

# Reflections

......................................................................

......................................................................

......................................................................

......................................................................

......................................................................

......................................................................

......................................................................

......................................................................

......................................................................

......................................................................

......................................................................

......................................................................

# Reflections

...........................................................................

...........................................................................

...........................................................................

...........................................................................

...........................................................................

...........................................................................

...........................................................................

...........................................................................

...........................................................................

...........................................................................

...........................................................................

...........................................................................

# Reflections

# Reflections

........................................................................

........................................................................

........................................................................

........................................................................

........................................................................

........................................................................

........................................................................

........................................................................

........................................................................

........................................................................

........................................................................

........................................................................

........................................................................

# Reflections

.......................................................................

.......................................................................

.......................................................................

.......................................................................

.......................................................................

.......................................................................

.......................................................................

.......................................................................

.......................................................................

.......................................................................

.......................................................................

.......................................................................

# Reflections

..............................................................................

..............................................................................

..............................................................................

..............................................................................

..............................................................................

..............................................................................

..............................................................................

..............................................................................

..............................................................................

..............................................................................

..............................................................................

..............................................................................

..............................................................................

# ABOUT THE AUTHOR

CHERIE DAWN CARR is the author of seven books centered on healing through intimate relationships with the natural world. She is a tribal member of the Choctaw Nation of Oklahoma. She writes as Lighthorse to honor the unheard voices of her ancestors, who were forcibly removed from our homelands via the first of many Trails of Tears. Pixie Lighthorse currently resides in the Pacific Northwest.